PROPHETIC
IDENTITY
and
DESTINY

Cover design by: Sara Young
Cover photo by: Monty Nuss

ISBN: 978-1-964794-69-3   1 2 3 4 5 6 7 8 9 10

Printed in the United States of America

WHAT PEOPLE ARE SAYING ABOUT
PROPHETIC IDENTITY *and* DESTINY

Dr. Timothy Bagwell is in a category and a class all by himself. His passionate delivery, and personal character have catapulted the spiritual growth of The Potter's House of Dallas and all other ministries that have availed themselves of his expertise. I am confident in advising all serious-minded Christians to saturate themselves with his wisdom. *Prophetic Identity and Destiny* is a call from God as He uses Dr. Bagwell as His bugle.

—Bishop T.D. Jakes Sr.
The Potter's House of Dallas, Inc.
CEO, TDJ Enterprises, LLP

A prophet, pastor, and teacher, Tim Bagwell literally exemplifies the empowerment of the call of God on a believer's life. Knowing Tim Bagwell, and my time ministering in their church in Denver made me realize that he is a great man with an anointed church. They reflect Tim's anointed ministry, his scholarly insights into God's Word, and his passionate love and vision.

—The late Oral Roberts

I was excited to write an endorsement for Dr. Timothy Bagwell and his book, *Prophetic Identity and Destiny*. Dr. Bagwell is qualified to write about the prophetic. He has demonstrated a lifetime of hearing from God and faithfully speaking what he has heard. Many in the body of Christ believe in the prophetic but don't consistently participate in it. Sometimes the prophetic needs an advocate. Tim is that!

I could say a lot about the book but let me instead say something about the author.

I know Tim as a friend, the pastor of an outstanding megachurch, a dedicated husband to a beautiful wife, a successful father to two sons who have followed him in the ministry, and a proud grandfather. He's also a pretty good golfer! All of these things are important to know because a man who purports to prophetically "speak for God" needs to have both feet on the ground. I'm really excited to see the impact that this important work will have on the lives of many around the world. I believe you will feel informed and inspired by reading this book.

—Mike Hayes
Founder
Covenant Church, Dallas, TX

In this generation, the Lord has raised up strategic leaders that time, testing, and godly compassion to empower the Church have equipped to face the challenges of this fast-paced information age in which we live. Tim Bagwell is one of those rare individuals whose gifted spirit, transparent character, and integrity are a welcome breath of fresh air. I highly recommend his relevant and timely message to all those who desire truth. It lays down principles = destined to impact your life and the world around you.

—The late Dr. Myles Munroe
Bahamas Faith Ministries

PROPHETIC IDENTITY *and* DESTINY

YOU ARE **WHO GOD SAYS** YOU ARE

TIM BAGWELL

AVAIL

I dedicate this book to my wife,
Gayla Jean Bagwell.

For fifty years, you have stood by me and helped
me in every way to accomplish what God has
called me to do. I could have never succeeded
without your prayers, creativity, wisdom, discern-
ment, and constant encouragement. You have
heard me preach every thought captured in this
book and have constantly affirmed that the Lord
anointed these words for His people. A simple
"thank you" does not seem to capture all I feel
in my heart for what you have done, sacrificed,
and meant to me in this marathon we have run
together. When God gave you to me, He knew
exactly who I would need in all seasons of my life.

CONTENTS

FOREWORD

There are voices, and then there are trumpets. Pastor Tim Bagwell is a trumpet—a clarion sound in an era clouded by ambiguity, compromise, and spiritual apathy. His words do not echo—they pierce. His revelations do not merely inform—they transform. And this book you hold in your hands is no exception.

For over four decades, Pastor Bagwell has been a prophetic voice to the body of Christ, a general in the Lord's army, and a relentless champion of truth, fire, and supernatural breakthrough. He has walked with kings and prayed with paupers, preached to multitudes, and pastored individuals, but through it all, one thing has remained consistent: his unwavering commitment to the power of God and the authority of His Word.

This book is not just a collection of thoughts or theological insights—it is a prophetic blueprint. It is a spiritual war cry calling the Church back to power, back to purpose, and back to the presence of the Almighty. Pastor Bagwell writes with the weight of experience and the breath of the Spirit. Each chapter carries the unmistakable signature of someone who has not only studied the fire but has walked through it and emerged with a double portion.

In these pages, you will find revelation that will awaken your spirit, confront your complacency, and call you higher. You will be reminded that the same power that raised Jesus from the dead is not a historical relic—it is alive, active, and accessible to every believer who dares to believe. This book will challenge you to live boldly, preach unapologetically, pray fervently, and lead courageously.

I believe this is more than a book—it is a mantle. A transfer. An invitation to step into the deep things of God and to become a carrier of glory in a world desperate for light.

To my friend, Pastor Tim Bagwell—thank you. Thank you for staying true. Thank you for being both voice and vessel. And thank you for once again delivering a message that the Church desperately needs to hear.

Now, reader, turn the page. But don't just read—receive.

Let the fire fall.

Pastor Samuel Rodriguez

INTRODUCTION

*But as the days of Noah were, so also will
the coming of the Son of Man be.*
—Matthew 24:37

T he Old Testament accounts of Joseph's life, Israel's deliverance from Egypt and Pharaoh, and Israel's ultimate conquest of the Promised Land are more than just historical accounts. I believe they are prophetic oracles—a road map showing today's church how to possess our divine destinies.

We either choose to accept a limited vision that is defined by our historical viewpoint or we embrace an eagle-eyed perspective that is prophetic. Proverbs 29:18 states that "where there is no vision, the people perish" (KJV). The word *vision* speaks of prophetic utterance and revelation.[1] The word *perish* means to be unrestrained and run wild.[2] In the true power of the prophetic, we define our future by what God has said, rather than what the darkness, void, and chaos of our yesterdays seem to dictate. Many times, the past declares

---

1 Blue Letter Bible, s.v. "ḥāzôn," accessed April 4, 2024, https://www.blueletterbible.org/lexicon/h2377/kjv/wlc/0-1/.
2 Blue Letter Bible, s.v. "pāra," accessed April 4, 2024, https://www.blueletterbible.org/lexicon/h6544/kjv/wlc/0-1/.

what we can't do, solely on the basis of historical limitations. The prophetic reveals that all things are obtainable because our future is written by God, not our circumstances.

The beloved apostle John states in Revelation 3:18 that God anoints our eyes with an eye salve so that we may see. To truly see requires the anointing that enables us to see beyond the natural, into the spiritual. This anointed eyesight perceives our God-given future from afar. Job 39:27-29 explains that the eagle lives in a high place and sees its prey off in the distance. Joseph saw his destiny thirteen years ahead of possessing it. The nation of Israel had been given prophetic insight many generations before they crossed the Jordan.

God has done the same for us. According to 1 Timothy 1:18, we have been given personal prophecies to "war a good warfare" (KJV). The divinely spoken "God said"s of our personal lives prepare us to war against the darkness, void, and chaos that the enemy continually puts in our paths.

During the past five decades of full-time ministry, I have come to realize that we, God's people, are embracing the prophetic in a euphoric way that dulls our awareness of His intent. His words encourage us, but they are given as a compass and weapon to ensure that we possess our God-given calls and destinies. God is not a predictor; He is a Creator. He is not predicting our tomorrows but creating our future. He did not predict the light in Genesis 1:3; He spoke the light into existence.

Today, your destiny is being hand-created by your creative God. In a world immersed in darkness, void, and chaos, there is only one way to see darkness become light, emptiness become overflow, and chaos become righteous order: we must allow God to speak into us and through us to reverse the schemes of Satan's kingdom.

In this life, there will be battles and victories. The victories will be glorious, but the battles seem to come in like a flood. Our church recently received a prophetic word about the flood in Noah's day, and it helped us to see the story in a fresh way. Here is that word, as Pastor Marco Peixoto of Rio de Janeiro, Brazil, delivered it:

> *Pastor Bagwell,*
> *This word is in me, and it keeps stirring within me, and I have to speak this to you and the church. When the floodwaters came, they covered the earth, and they destroyed everything. But the same water that destroyed the whole earth is the same water that elevated the ark. In 1 Peter, it says that Noah was saved by the water of that generation. God says to say to you, Pastor Bagwell and Word of Life Christian Center, everything that contributed to bring a flooding of difficulties and problems is changing to a time of elevation and strength. The flood is now the source of elevation and renewed power for a totally new season of revival. God is going to elevate this generation!*

Of course, we know how the flood ended in Noah's day. But Noah and his family never saw the ending in print. They had to believe their way through the ordeal. As the waters continued to rise, so did their trepidation. They were shut up in an ark with hundreds of animals. They knew that people were perishing all around them. And they had no idea where the ark would end up. Yes, Noah trusted God, but staying focused through the flood took faith.

The prophecy our church received did not ignore the challenges Noah and his family faced. It simply reminded us of the miracle within the flood that we often overlook. We need to remember that in Scripture, rain is a symbol of God speaking from heaven, to and for His people. Whatever He speaks is a blessing, as Scripture explains:

For as the rain comes down, and the snow from heaven,
And do not return there,
But water the earth,
And make it bring forth and bud,
That it may give seed to the sower
And bread to the eater,
So shall My word be that goes forth from My mouth;
It shall not return to Me void,
But it shall accomplish what I please,
And it shall prosper in the thing for which I sent it.
—Isaiah 55:10-11

When God speaks, His words lift His people to a higher place while they destroy the works of the enemy. When He speaks healing, people are made whole, and the spirit of infirmity is destroyed. When He speaks peace, chaos leaves. When He speaks about His protection, fear must go. God's Word is alive, active, and powerful (Hebrews 4:12). What He says redeems, restores, and removes the remnants of darkness.

The same devastating waters that wiped the earth clean of wildlife, structures, and much of humanity also safely deposited an ark with eight souls and hundreds of animals on the sixteen-thousand-foot mountain called Ararat. It is interesting that *Ararat* refers to the place of curse reversal, and the number eight represents new beginnings. Amid the chaos and carnage of the flood, God lifted Noah's family and their cargo to a place of curse reversal and a fresh start!

The prophecy our church received is a reminder that God is using the world's current chaos to elevate His people. The word is still resonating at our church, especially because it wasn't only for us. The floodwaters that seem poised to take *you* out will carry *you* to a high place of safety where your perspective will be elevated, and your vision will expand. With God, what looks like your downfall can become your arising! The waters that are disturbing your peace can deliver you out of the past and into what God has next.

Peter explained it this way: "When once the longsuffering of God waited in the days of Noah, while the ark was a preparing, wherein few, that is, eight souls were saved by water" (1 Peter 3:20, KJV). Pay close attention to the wording: eight souls were saved—not from the water but by the water. When circumstances go haywire or the enemy rises up against you, remember Noah's testimony. When you are tempted to be afraid, anticipate your Ararat, which is your deliverance and new beginning. Worry will provoke you; it is part of the fallen human nature. But you have a new nature, and deliverance is yours in Christ.

We are in a hard season. That is the reason I chose to write this book. I have preached more sermons than I can count, and I have written my share of books. But I believe we are at a crossroads: will we remain restrained by historical perspectives or soar to new heights because of our prophetic perspective?

SKIP THE MAINTENANCE WALK

So, what must we do? Let's start with what not to do. Let's not quit before reaching our God-given destinies. Let's not be controlled by fear or doubt. And let's not be complacent. Too many Christians are leading a "maintenance walk." They're clinging to yesterday's blessings and parking there. I am convinced that this is what kept Moses's generation from reaching their destiny. They had been oppressed for so long that they developed a slave mentality and became accustomed to failure. This bred the maintenance mentality that tricked them into settling for less than what God had in mind.

This mindset is common today. Fear and exhaustion have driven many people to retreat to their comfort zones. Amid all the shaking, they want safety and security above all. Then, they wonder why they have become apathetic about the things of God. Let me point out the obvious: as Christians, we are to live under the influence of the Holy Spirit. The tenacity with which we follow Him is up to us. We get to choose whether to coast or accelerate. The choice is both personal and corporate. If you choose to be satisfied with second best in this life, there isn't much God can do for you. He can show you the greater thing, but if you are content to do without, He will not violate your will. He will not force you to live in His blessing or possess His promise.

Maintenance walkers miss out on the best part because fearful people are not possessors. They become passive survivors who are satisfied to stagnate. Yes! What God did for us "back then" was wonderful, but it's in the past. The future is up ahead. God is still speaking and leading us into greater things than we realize. He has something fresh to say to His church, and we need to rise up and receive it.

There is a verse that sums up this idea. I have shared it a thousand times. Maybe you have heard it a thousand times. But don't let familiarity dull your hearing. God speaks in the freshness of *now*. His Word is "living and powerful" (Hebrews 4:12). Every time He says something, there is more to understand. So, let this verse from the apostle Paul enter your heart and obliterate every shred of maintenance mentality: "Brethren, I do not count myself to have apprehended; but one thing *I do*, forgetting those things which are behind and reaching forward to those things which are ahead, I press toward the goal for the prize of the upward call of God in Christ Jesus" (Philippians 3:13-14).

This is not the time to be passive but the time to advance. God has never stopped moving in the earth, not even in times like ours, when profound and destabilizing shifts are almost everyday occurrences. God is not moved by any of it, but He is moving!

UNDERSTAND THE SHIFT

I believe we are witnessing God Himself orchestrating a worldwide shift and setting the scene for a fresh move of His Spirit (see Hebrews 12:25-26). This is a new hour in God. The sun is rising, and our Ararat—the place of curse reversal—is ahead. The season of maintenance is over. It is time to take our places and be proactive.

Do you remember what the Lord told Joshua after Moses died? God said, "Moses My servant is dead. Now therefore, arise" (Joshua 1:2). Perhaps more than anybody loved Moses, Joshua loved him and mourned his passing. However, God indicated that the time of mourning was over, and it was "go time." Israel was now to possess what God had promised. But to possess it, *they had to arise.* They had a new leader, but God's word to them had never changed. It was time to get up and possess what God had prophesied years earlier.

I believe it is time for us to arise. We have all suffered some kind of loss in recent years, but it is time to move forward. We cannot possess our destiny while mourning our past. When God says, "Go," we must arise and defeat our enemies. Unless we do God's bidding, the darkness will stand firm. Bigotry and hatred will increase. Drug and sex trafficking, sexual perversion, violence, and poverty will escalate. No political or military task force can resolve these matters. When we, as God's people, become proactive, we will deal with them spiritually. They will be stopped when we use our authority and break the power of the evil spirits that are driving people toward the darkness.

This is not a time for obsessing over the evil that surrounds us. It is time to rise up and bring deliverance to those who are bound. It is time to move out of Egypt's sphere of influence and start marching toward our prophetic promise. It will take more than religious rhetoric and verses from a social media post to resist satanic opposition. We need more than that not to be fooled by the enemy or the nature of the floodwaters. It is going to take prophetic revelation, the power of the blood, and an anointed lifestyle to reverse the curse and conquer our adversary. I pray that as you read these pages, you will allow my fifty-plus years of ministry to stir the determination in you to be the unique creation God has called you to be. Your God-given spiritual DNA and identity are waiting to be released to impact the world around you.

Remember . . . *you are who God says you are*!

THE FLOOD OF HIS SPIRIT

Obviously, the flood we are discussing is not a physical flood. Precipitation in the earth's atmosphere is not the issue. What I am talking about is an outpouring of the Holy Ghost. When it comes, God will break the back of the spirit of evil that is trying to corrupt our planet. He will rain down His power and presence and destroy the things of darkness. The floodwaters will ultimately wipe out infirmities, deceptive spirits, heaviness, diseases, depression, and every ugly thing that has existed since the fall of man. The waters will not destroy us; they will deliver us!

This is where I believe we are. I am convinced that God is behind the shaking we are witnessing, and it is moving us closer to His ultimate plan. His promises have not changed, but we might need to change in order to fully embrace and receive them. For example, we cannot expect God's intentions to be fulfilled in the absence of difficulty. Warfare is a fact of the Christian life. But know this: Jesus has not thrown us to the wolves or left us adrift in the flood. He is not perplexed or running late. He has not deserted us in our wilderness or forgotten what He has promised. He will arise and go before us. He is moving even now. And He is taking us to higher ground.

Are you ready?

Part 1

PROPHETIC PROMISE
and
THE BLOOD

Chapter 1

THE PROMISE AND THE PROBLEM

Every place that the sole of your foot will tread
upon I have given you, as I said to Moses.
—Joshua 1:3

As Christ's disciples, we are people of the promise. However, before we can possess the promise, we must understand it, embrace it, and posture ourselves for its fulfillment. Even when we are sure we are trusting Him, we can make two overarching mistakes: The first is trying to figure out what we want in life instead of what God wants. The second is being too easily satisfied with something less than God's best.

Our natural minds can't quite comprehend the fullness of what God wants to do through our lives. Only He sees the complete picture, and only He can point the right way forward. We can try to build our lives around what our natural minds think, only to miss out on something infinitely better. *Nothing* can compare with what God has in mind.

So, let's prepare our hearts, first by learning from the pitfalls God's people have encountered on their way to His promises.

PASSIVE SURVIVOR OR ACTIVE POSSESSOR?

The path to the promise won't always be smooth. You will encounter enemies, and you will need to drive them out. I'm not talking about people but about mindsets and other obstacles that get in the way. We are called to experience God's signs, wonders, and miracles, much like those the Israelites experienced in the wilderness. They crossed the Red Sea on a road that was hidden from view. They drank water from a rock. For forty years, their clothing did not wear out, and their feet did not blister or swell. And in the middle of the desert, they never lacked for food (Psalm 77:19; Exodus 17:1-7; Deuteronomy 8:4; Exodus 16:1-35).

Despite all they witnessed, however, the Israelites struggled to trust God. When Moses sent twelve spies to scout out the Promised Land (Numbers 13), ten of them returned with a bad report. Instead of focusing on the richness of the land, they were intimidated by the giants who lived there. Full of fear, these spies complained that they were no match for the giants. When the people heard their report, they joined in the fear and fell to pieces.

The giants weren't the problem. The real issue was the mindset the Israelites developed during their history of enslavement. Four hundred years of bondage had beaten them down and eroded their identity as God's chosen people. Now, with their freedom already won, their maintenance mentality erupted in full-blown passive survivor mode, making them intimidated and unwilling to fight for the promise. This mindset would eventually separate them from their destiny and cause them to die in the wilderness, without a glimpse of their Promised Land.

Possessing our destiny is not a passive act. We are to be active possessors of the promise. That means facing our enemies and driving them out. We cannot do this unless we trust what God has said and then act on our trust. The price of passivity is the difference between living in fear and living in faith, and without faith, it is impossible to please God (Hebrews 11:6). Passivity will cost us the promise! Too many in the church want God's blessings while they continue in their old habits. Sin is sin, whether it's a passive mindset, an ungodly lifestyle, a refusal to walk in wisdom, a careless approach to finances, or a tendency to distrust or disbelieve God. Embracing sin will make us a generation of compromisers, like the older generation of Israelites. They did not possess what God prepared for them because compromisers never do.

Compromise and the anointing are incompatible. Compromise will not break yokes of bondage or heal the sick. It gives no hope to husbands and wives whose marriages are failing. And it cannot deliver the addicted from their torment. That requires the touch from God that causes all enemies to flee. But God's touch is sacred and *without* compromise. En route to our prophetic promise, we need to keep our hearts and minds fixed on whatever is compatible with the anointing— that which is true, noble, just, pure, lovely, and "of good report" (Philippians 4:8).

That is what Joshua and Caleb did during the Israelites' trek in the wilderness. They kept their hearts and minds fixed on what God had said. They believed His promise was good. They knew He could be trusted, and they were determined to actively possess the land. When Moses sent them with the other ten spies to scout out Canaan, he told them what to look for. He said, "See what the land is like: whether the people who dwell in it are strong or weak, few or many; whether the land they dwell in is good or bad; whether the cities they inhabit are like camps or strongholds" (Numbers 13:18-19). Then, he told them to "be of good courage" (v. 20).

When the spies reported back to Moses, they all admitted that the land flowed with milk and honey, but ten of them hedged and made excuses. "Nevertheless," they said, "the people who dwell in the land *are* strong; the cities *are* fortified and very large; moreover we saw the descendants of Anak there" (Numbers 13:28). Their defeatist report was a laundry list of everything they believed they could not do.

Caleb saw everything the ten spies described but interpreted it through the lens of a "God said." He wasn't discouraged by how things looked or how the other spies whimpered. He "quieted the people before Moses, and said, 'Let us go up at once and take possession, for we are well able to overcome it'" (Numbers 13:30).

Caleb saw everything the ten spies described but interpreted it through the lens of a "God said."

The ten passive-survivor spies protested. "We are not able to go up against the people," they said, "for they are stronger than we" (Numbers 13:31). They knew exactly what God had promised. They experienced the same signs, wonders, and miracles that Caleb and Joshua did. They knew that God had designated the territory to be theirs, but to them, the giants were greater than God's promise. Without realizing it, they disqualified themselves from entering the land.

IT TAKES A MIRACLE

If I have learned anything, it is this: the only way to enter into your prophetic promise is through a miracle from God. After Moses died and Joshua became the Israelites' leader, it was time to enter the land. That meant crossing the Jordan at flood stage (Joshua 3:15), which would take a miracle.

God told Joshua, "You shall command the priests who bear the ark of the covenant, saying, 'When you have come to the edge of the water of the Jordan, you shall stand in the Jordan'" (Joshua 3:8).

Why did the priests have to stand in the water? To wait for God's miracle! He promised:

> *"As soon as the soles of the feet of the priests who bear the ark of the LORD, the Lord of all the earth, shall rest in the waters of the Jordan . . . the waters of the Jordan shall be cut off, the waters that come down from upstream, and they shall stand as a heap." —Joshua 3:13*

There are many things you can do to possess your promise, but there are some things you *cannot* do. You can sanctify yourself. You can break loose from where you are. You can decide to follow God's glory and respect His leadership. But you cannot part the Jordan. Only God can do that.

You cannot possess your prophetic promises without His supernatural touch.

When passivity rules you, you become oblivious to God's greatness. Even the parting of the waters, which should incite joy and gratitude, can stir fear because you know giants await you on the other side. The Israelites lost sight of God's promise and omnipotence. They had themselves on their minds and could only say, "Our enemies are bigger than us." They had no intention of crossing the Jordan unless God first wiped out their adversaries.

Do you see the conundrum their thinking created? They had God's plan backward. He promised to open the waters so they could enter the land and drive out the giants. He wasn't handing them over to their enemies; He was empowering them for victory. If you are struggling with the passivity the maintenance mindset creates, you need to take stock. As long as you hide on the wrong side of the Jordan, the giants will never leave. But if you trust God and cross over, He will drive them out and rid you of them for good.

Listen to what Joshua told the people:

"By this you shall know that the living God is among you, and that He will without fail *drive out from before you the Canaanites and the Hittites and the Hivites and the Perizzites and the Girgashites and the Amorites and the Jebusites: Behold, the ark of the covenant of the Lord of all the earth is crossing over before you into the Jordan." —Joshua 3:10-11 (emphasis added)*

In other words, "You will not take the land without a fight, but you will take the land." God will go before you. If you obsess over your enemies, you will never obtain what He promised and never become the person He intends you to be. But if you let God handle the enemies in the land, He will do it, without fail.

DON'T BACK DOWN

Satan was perfectly satisfied with the Israelites living in God's provision because maintenance-minded Israelites camped out in the desert presented no threat to his kingdom. What he feared were the conquerors—the Joshuas and Calebs who were willing to believe God, cross the Jordan, and possess the land God said was theirs. These possessors threatened Satan's dominion.

Israel's enemies were enjoying the land of milk and honey and had no intention of handing it over. To protect their residency, the enemy sought to dampen the Israelites' desire for the promise. Did you get that? *The devil wanted God's people to see His promise as being too difficult to obtain.* He knew that if they backed away, they would miss their destiny in God and ultimately surrender their identity as His people. Then, they would never threaten Satan's kingdom again.

The devil is strategic. He concentrates on stopping the conquerors who are committed to acting on the divine promise. He focuses on silencing the prayer warriors and tries to keep the evangelists from evangelizing. He discourages exhorters from exhorting, teachers from teaching, pastors from pastoring, and prophets from prophesying. He wants to prevent

God's people from entering the fullness of their callings. He knows that as long as he keeps them satisfied with existing on the wrong side of the Jordan, his kingdom is safe.

Satan's argument is flawed, and Joshua and Caleb knew it. Sidestepping the battle cannot provide the safety and security we crave, and it certainly gives God no glory. It only exposes our failure to discern the spiritual landscape and the power of God and His promises. Will there be battles? Yes. But even those who thought they had withdrawn from the fight have wars to wage. The less willing we are to fight, the less there is to win. But the greater the battle, the greater the victory.

When you obey God, you will be safer on the frontlines than in your hiding place. The enemy might heat up the furnace seven times hotter than usual (Daniel 3:19), but God will get there before you. He will be *in* the fire to deliver you *from* the fire.

I don't know about you, but I am determined to cross over into the fertile valleys of my prophetic promise. I want to enjoy the bounty there and share it with others. I know there are battles ahead. I am counting on it! But there is nothing to fear. If I am there in obedience to God, He will make me a giant killer. And when I cross over, He will prove that He is with me by giving me the victory.

Don't back down or settle for what the devil offers. Be willing to fight for your blessing. This is not a rehearsal. You are fighting for your promised land, your children and grandchildren, your loved ones, your home, and your blessings—and they are worth the fight!

The less willing you are to fight, the less there is to win. But the greater the battle, the greater the victory.

GRASSHOPPER MENTALITY

The devil is sly. He deceived the Israelites and incited them to doubt themselves and God's promises, and he did it through mind games. The demonic deception was evident in what the fearful spies said when Caleb refuted their report and encouraged Israel to take the land:

> *"The land through which we have gone as spies is a land that devours its inhabitants, and all the people whom we saw in it are men of great stature. There we saw the giants (the descendants of Anak came from the giants);* and we were like grasshoppers in our own sight, and so we were in their sight.*
> —Numbers 13:32-33 (emphasis added)*

Remember that the spies had seen with their own eyes a land flowing with milk and honey. They also brought back grapes, pomegranates, and figs from Canaan (Numbers 13:23). They had arrived there "in the season of the first ripe grapes" (Numbers 13:20), so in the Valley of Eschol, they "cut down a branch with one cluster of grapes" (Numbers 13:23). That one cluster required the strength of two men to carry it!

The land they visited was fruitful. However, the ten fearful spies described it as a land that "devours its inhabitants" (Numbers 13:32). Not only did they see themselves as grasshoppers, but they claimed that the Canaanites also saw them that way (Numbers 13:33). The passage doesn't describe any interaction between the giants and the Israelites. It is possible that some name-calling occurred. It is also possible that the Israelites were intimidated without a word being exchanged. Either way, God's chosen people had no business seeing themselves as grasshoppers.

The grasshopper mentality betrayed the Israelites' identity as God's people and showed the enemy that he had gotten inside their heads. He talked them out of what God said was theirs and tricked them out of being possessors. Taking possession of their destiny as God's people would be impossible unless they came out of the grasshopper mindset. Until they broke free, they were not capable of enjoying God's best for them.

The lesson from Israel's story is clear. It takes a proactive spiritual mindset to possess your prophetic promise. I'm talking about the mindset of the possessor who believes the promise of God is assured and the only real grasshoppers are His enemies. As a possessor, you press for God's best, believing that you can conquer any and every adversary that tries to come between you and your destiny.

The devil is sly. He talked the Israelites out of what God said was theirs and tricked them out of being possessors.

"KILL" THE "KINGS"

Once Israel entered the territory God had given them, He spoke to Joshua about the reason they were there: to take possession of the land He prophesied was theirs. The land's inhabitants were already shaken by the Israelites' miraculous crossing of the Jordan. In Jericho, the people locked down their city "because of the children of Israel" so that "none went out, and none came in" (Joshua 6:1). They were worried sick about what God and His people would do next.

That's when the Lord told Joshua, "See! I have given Jericho into your hand, its king, and the mighty men of valor" (Joshua 6:2). God was giving Joshua a strategy of warfare that he would repeat many times in taking the territory. It involved *how* they would go about it. The territory was not going to drop into Israel's lap. They would have to fight for it. But God knew how the battle in Jericho would go, and He said, "Don't worry, Joshua. I gave you Jericho's king and its mighty men of valor. Jericho is yours."

In other words, taking Jericho meant first taking its king and his mighty men of valor. Once they fell, the territory would fold. This strategy was not new. When God called Moses to lead Israel out of Egypt, He sent Moses to confront Egypt's king, its political and spiritual head known as Pharaoh (Exodus 3:10). He was Egypt's power center, the man who held God's people captive. You could say he was the pharaoh of their circumstances. Before Israel could break free, God would have to break down Pharaoh and the mighty men who served him.

Pharaoh did not go down easily, but He did go down—to the bottom of the Red Sea. Before that happened, however, he oppressed the Israelites even more. Moses tried to encourage them with a word from God, but the people "did not heed Moses, because of anguish of spirit and cruel bondage" (Exodus 6:9). They were like some of the people you and I talk to today—they had suffered long and hard and could not hear the truth. The Israelites had lost hope too many times and were now captives of their despair—until God closed the Red Sea's parted waters over the chariots of Pharaoh and his mighty men of valor. When Egypt's headship came down, Israel was finally free.

Warfare always precedes a victory. And always, you have to confront the power—the "king"—that is enforcing your captivity. Remember that "the weapons of our warfare are not carnal," and we wrestle "against principalities, against powers, against the rulers of the darkness of this age, against spiritual hosts of wickedness in the heavenly places" (Ephesians 6:12; see 2 Corinthians 10:4). Moses had to deal with Pharaoh, and Joshua would have to deal with the kings who ruled throughout Canaan and tried to block Israel from the various territories. These kings opposed God by standing between His people and His promise to them.

Defeating the kings did not happen overnight. Israel had to take possession of their prophetic promise piece by piece. That meant taking out one king after another until every territory had fallen to them. In all, Joshua had to kill thirty-one kings and all their mighty men of valor! (See Joshua 12:24.) That's a lot of battles won. You could say that Israel experienced a winning streak!

KNOW WHO YOU ARE FIGHTING

Moses and Joshua understood the battle and knew who they were fighting. God sent them to deal with the influencers—the ones who ruled their respective territories and decided who could come, who could go, and who could be free. The same is true in the spiritual sense today. If you want to fulfill your call and destiny, you have to take down the "king" who wants to keep you out. If you want to rescue your children, friends, loved ones, neighbors, cities, and nation from the grip of the enemy, you must kill the wicked influence that controls them. This is not a battle against flesh and blood but against principalities, powers, and other wicked entities that are warring in the heavenly places (Ephesians 6:12).

Many Christians today are overly polite to the devil and act like they're afraid to violate his "rights." Joshua had no such concern and showed neither respect nor mercy for the thirty-one kings he conquered. First, he utterly humiliated them; then, he saw to their execution. It was not a matter of bloodthirst but of obedience to God, who was leading His people into the fulfillment of His will.

We must be willing to destroy every spiritual king who has tried to build strongholds in our lives and our loved ones' lives, including strongholds of jealousy, immorality, depression, and gender dysphoria. Like Joshua instructed his men to do, we are to put these "kings" under our feet (Joshua 10:24), not as a work of our own flesh but by God's Spirit. Remember: people are not our enemies, and *our* fleshly power will not produce the victory.

Do you believe that you can't do it? Does the battle seem too big? It isn't—not if you wage good warfare by faith. Destroying spiritual kings requires faith in God. We get that faith by hearing and reading God's Word. Romans 10:17 says that "faith comes by hearing, and hearing by the word of God."

Always, the battle is the Lord's. And always, the victory is won in the Spirit, by faith in Jesus Christ.

Like Joshua instructed his men to do, we are to put wicked spiritual kings under our feet (Joshua 10:24).

FAITH FOR THE CALLING

Joshua needed confidence to slay the thirty-one enemy kings. But his confidence was not in himself, his soldiers, or the priests and Levites. They could not overcome such strong enemies. Joshua's confidence was in his God and in what God told him:

> *"No man shall be able to stand before you all the days of your life; as I was with Moses, so I will be with you. I will not leave you nor forsake you. Be strong and of good courage, for to this people you shall divide as an inheritance the land which I swore to their fathers to give them. Only be strong and very courageous, that you may observe to do according to all the law which Moses My servant commanded you; do not turn from it to the right hand or to the left, that you may prosper wherever you go." —Joshua 1:5-7*

Joshua trusted the God who is greater than any enemy and greater than all enemies combined. Because of his trust, Joshua overcame fear and grief and fought courageously, knowing (1) the battle was the Lord's and (2) the battle was won.

Have you ever won a battle and thought, *I just got lucky*?

I think we all have! For some reason, we seem almost surprised when we win. But should we be? We are not destined for defeat. We are not called to live under the devil's yoke.

We are called to break free of all bondage. Being thankful for every victory the Lord gives us is appropriate. But let's remember that winning is part of our inheritance. God did not intend for us to be poverty-stricken, diseased, mentally impaired, or infirmed in any way. He did not intend for us to be confused, depressed, or downtrodden. He is a God of total victory. He created us to rise up in the power of the Holy Spirit, put the devil under our feet, and keep him there. We have been empowered through Christ to enjoy victory—not a "lucky" win now and then but continuing conquests as He leads.

Keep God's promises before you. Remind yourself of them often. Be determined to drive out every spiritual king and mighty man of valor and take back what is rightfully yours. The fight is *not* too big. You are *not* a grasshopper in God's eyes. When you are doing what He has called you to do, going where He has called you to go, and saying what He has called you to say, you will face opposition. But fear not; He is supplying your every need (Philippians 4:19), and as His child, you have authority on the earth. Tell the devil to step aside. Then, move into your promised land.

THE PROMISE IS WORTH THE PROBLEM

Following each chapter is a section like this one that is designed to anchor a thought, a change, or a bridge to what is ahead. Invest a few minutes in your present that will help to shape your future. You won't regret it.

If a battle precedes every victory, you not only need a battle plan but a victory plan that might include (metaphorically) "killing" some "kings" when the battle is over.

Which "kings" are you fighting, and how will you "kill" them?

Chapter 2

THE KEYS TO POSSESSION

"Have I not commanded you? Be strong and of good courage; do not be afraid, nor be dismayed, for the LORD your God is with you wherever you go."
—Joshua 1:9

We have just seen how promises and temptations travel together as God's people move toward their destinies. The pitfalls they have encountered in history stand as warnings. Now, let's focus on some important keys to staying alert, sober, and positioned to possess our promised land, whether our circumstances seem favorable or not.

WAKE UP TO THE WARFARE

Before the United States entered World War II, military intelligence repeatedly warned that Pearl Harbor was vulnerable and would likely be attacked. Military leaders glossed over the warnings and the vulnerabilities of the naval installation. At a critical moment in history, they failed to recognize the coming battle and misunderstood the mindset of a very determined enemy. Their miscalculation had tragic consequences. When Japan attacked Pearl Harbor, 2,403 lives were lost, and nineteen US ships—all easy targets—were damaged or destroyed.[3]

Much of today's church has a similar mindset. They do not acknowledge the battle in the heavenlies and are unprepared for the spiritual warfare God's Word describes. This blissful ignorance of our place on the battlefield exposes people and churches to the enemy's attacks. We have received all the intelligence we need: the dark kingdom's determination is spelled out in the Scriptures. The first key to taking our territory is to recognize the battle. There is no excuse for us to be easy targets.

Satan continually wages war against God and His people. He is happy to attack your marriage and undermine your morality. While you are "asleep," He strategizes to steal your children and your health and seeks ways to control everything you hold dear in life. He's cunning and an expert at lulling you into a false sense of security by advancing incrementally and obscuring the larger picture. But remember God's warning: "Be sober, be vigilant; because your adversary the devil walks about like a roaring lion, seeking whom he may devour" (1 Peter 5:8).

"Seeking whom he may devour. . . ." Does that sound like a determined enemy to you? It does to me. However, God calls us to be even more determined. He says, "Resist [the devil],

---

3   National WWII Museum, "Remembering Pearl Harbor: A Pearl Harbor Fact Sheet," census.gov, accessed August 5, 2023, https://www.census.gov/history/pdf/pearl-harbor-fact-sheet-1.pdf, 1.

steadfast in the faith, knowing that the same sufferings are experienced by your brotherhood in the world" (1 Peter 5:9). God is telling us what ought to be plain enough: we and all our brothers and sisters in Christ are on the battlefield, whether we acknowledge it or not. As members of Christ's body, each of us has a part in this warfare. The attacks we experience are common to all and have been so throughout the ages.

The enemy's tactics are straightforward. Jesus said, "The thief does not come except to steal, and to kill, and to destroy." But Jesus also said, "I have come that they may have life, and that they may have it more abundantly" (John 10:10). The devil is powerless against the life Christ offers. Yet, you and I both know that enemy attacks come, and some cause harm. I don't want to overgeneralize, but I believe that a lack of awareness accounts for many of our losses. Too many of us don't believe spiritual warfare is real until after the bombardment comes, and we cry, "Why, God? Why?"

That question is most likely to come from those who are maintaining instead of advancing. Remember, we are not called to be passive survivors. We are to be active possessors who are alert, engaged, and poised to move toward victory and the abundant life that God has prepared for us.

Satan is not waiting on the sidelines. He is never inactive. While we prepare our arguments and our social media posts, he storms our strongholds. Picking fights in the flesh will not do. The only warfare that counts is spiritual, and it's happening in the heavenlies. We must learn to gird our loins with truth, protect ourselves with the breastplate of righteousness, walk in the gospel of peace, extinguish Satan's fiery darts with the shield of faith, wear the helmet of salvation, wield the sword of the Spirit (the Word of God), and pray (Ephesians 6:14-18). These are "the weapons of our warfare" (2 Corinthians 10:4). They "are not carnal but mighty in God for pulling down strongholds" (2 Corinthians 10:4).

The only warfare that counts is spiritual, and it's happening in the heavenlies.

Your intellect and physical abilities will not conquer the enemies that stand between you and your prophetic promise. You will only be victorious by the revelation of the Holy Spirit, and that comes through the knowledge and understanding of God's Word. But knowing and understanding are not enough; you need to *stand* on His Word. That means using it like the sword that it is. Start believing and acting upon the knowledge you have gained during times of peace. Combine it with understanding and put both into action. This is what separates the medical student from the surgeon. The student has book knowledge; the surgeon knows how to use it and save lives.

Waking up to the warfare and using your sword are the differences between defeat and victory, between being a passive survivor who surrenders God's promises without a fight and an active possessor who occupies the land of milk and honey and enjoys its benefits.

RESPOND WITH OBEDIENCE AND PRAISE

Knowing how to respond to the battle is another key to possessing what God has prepared. Our human tendency is to fight fire with fire. But the only way to resist and overcome your spiritual enemies is to respond in obedience to God.

When King Jehoshaphat faced an overwhelming battle, he exemplified the kind of obedience that overcomes the odds. His military aides provided him with devastating military intelligence and told the king, "A great multitude is coming against you from beyond the sea, from Syria" (2 Chronicles 20:2). They were speaking of "the people of Moab with the people of Ammon, and others with them" who "came to battle against" Jehoshaphat (2 Chronicles 20:1).

When Jehoshaphat heard the news, fear gripped him. Yet, he made the right choice: He "set himself to seek the LORD, and proclaimed a fast throughout all Judah" (2 Chronicles 20:3). The people responded unanimously. They "gathered together to ask help from the LORD; and from all the cities of Judah they came to seek the LORD" (2 Chronicles. 20:4). The Lord responded to their cries, saying:

> *"Do not be afraid nor dismayed because of this great multitude, for the battle is not yours, but God's. . . . You will not need to fight in this battle. Position yourselves, stand still and see the salvation of the LORD."*
> —*2 Chronicles 20:15, 17*

God's order to stand still seemed unusual, but Jehoshaphat took it to heart. Judah would position themselves but not fight. Instead, they would worship God—on the battlefield! So:

> *When [Jehoshaphat] had consulted with the people, he appointed those who should sing to the LORD, and who should praise the beauty of holiness, as they went out before the army and were saying:*

"Praise the LORD, for His mercy endures forever."
—*2 Chronicles 20:21*

As Israel honored God and "began to sing and to praise" (2 Chronicles 20:22), an amazing thing happened: their enemies turned on themselves and killed one another. Logically and logistically, Jehoshaphat might have thought it more sensible to praise God after the battle was won or while Judah was striking down its enemies. But the king rejected what seemed sensible and sent out the praisers first. In response to Judah's obedience and praise, the Lord did exactly as He promised: He made them victorious.

Judah's success in this battle was not accomplished by charging the enemy or spilling their blood. It came by standing still, praising God, and awaiting His promised salvation. This posture was successful because they took it as an act of obedience. God said the battle was not theirs but His, and it was His to win.

The same is true today: the battle is not ours but God's, and the only path to victory is to follow His specific instructions in every situation. Our most powerful weapons are obedience, praise, and submission to His will, even when it seems to make no sense. As we obey and praise God, He will give us the victory and cause our enemies to destroy themselves.

Judah's success was not accomplished by charging the enemy or spilling their blood. It came by standing still, praising God, and awaiting His promised salvation.

Judah's obedience and praise not only saved them and glorified God; it also enriched God's people:

When Jehoshaphat and his people came to take away their spoil, they found among them an abundance of valuables on the dead bodies, and precious jewelry, which they stripped off for themselves, more than they could carry away; and they were three days gathering the spoil because there was so much.
—2 Chronicles 20:25 (KJV)

KNOW YOURSELF, RENEW YOUR MIND

A third key to possessing the promise is to know who you are. The story of the fearful spies in Numbers 13 and the entire Exodus account show that you cannot take the land until you settle your identity. The ten flustered spies were conflicted within themselves. God said they were His people and were empowered for the victory, but they insisted that they were grasshoppers! God did not give them that name. He created them in His image and likeness (Genesis 1:26-27). He knew their weaknesses, but He never characterized them as insects to be stepped on by giants. Quite the opposite! God promised that they would defeat the giants.

We are not grasshoppers, either. God's Word is very specific about our identity and leaves no room for confusion. Here is some of what He says about us:

First Peter 2:9 says, "You are a chosen generation, a royal priesthood, a holy nation, His own special people, that you may proclaim the praises of Him who called you out of darkness into His marvelous light."

Matthew 5:13-14 says, "You are the salt of the earth. . . . You are the light of the world."

Revelation 1:5-6 says, "Him who loved us and washed us from our sins in His own blood . . . has made us kings and priests to His God and Father."

In case any question about your identity still occupies your mind, ask yourself the question posed by the apostle Paul: "Do you not know that your body is the temple of the Holy Spirit who is in you, whom you have from God, and you are not your own?" (1 Corinthians 6:19)

What a profound statement—your human body is the temple of the Holy Spirit who lives within you! That should tell you who you are and *whose* you are. With that settled, you can believe God's promises and confidently receive them. You can believe in His protection against evil and destruction. You can trust His provision for all your needs. You can rely on His guidance and rest in the peace that only He can give. (See Psalms 91:10; Philippians 4:19; Psalms 73:24; and Isaiah 26:3.)

God's promises are fulfilled in faith. Isaiah 26:3 (emphasis added) says, "You will keep him in perfect peace, whose mind is stayed on You, *because he trusts in You.*" To have faith is to trust God. He gives us His Word, but we have to receive it and meditate on it, learning who we are and who He created us to be.

God's Word will renew your mind. Paul said, "Do not be conformed to this world, but be transformed by the renewing of your mind, that you may prove what is that good and acceptable and perfect will of God" (Romans 12:2). A renewed mind is set free from thoughts that oppose God's plan for your life. A renewed mind recognizes that you don't have to stay poor or live as a passive survivor. A renewed mind knows that being sick in the past doesn't mean you have to remain sick all your life.

When you meditate on God's Word and allow it to transform you, you can have the mind that "was also in Christ Jesus" (Philippians 2:5). Jesus Christ is the incarnate Word of God. When you renew your mind to the Word, the brilliance and power of Jesus Christ work in and through you. Then, you can move toward His promises and possess them. The battle is His, but the work of renewing your mind is yours.

Because God is truth, He can guarantee that His promise is good. What He cannot guarantee is that everyone will receive it. Moses's generation knew about their prophetic promise. It was the reason they followed Moses toward the Promised Land. God did not deliver them from Egypt so they could wander in the desert. He delivered them so they could possess the land of milk and honey. However, the generation that left Egypt never really wrapped their minds (their unrenewed minds) and hearts around what God said.

God did not fail those who died in the wilderness. His promise was good, and the active possessors—Joshua, Caleb, and the succeeding generation—received it. God guaranteed His people a good outcome. But He could not guarantee that every one of them would allow Him to transform their minds and self-image. A renewed mind was a choice that only they could make.

CHOOSE VICTORY

Victory is a choice. Satanic and demonic lies can cloud that choice. Many people miss God's best because someone or something has sown seeds of fear in their hearts, telling them the promise is too difficult to possess. This kind of slave mentality makes fear your master. Instead of being energized by God's prophetic promise to you, you lose the will to fight for what is yours. This is a profound loss because when God says that you can possess something, it is yours to possess. It doesn't matter how many giants are present. God will conquer every one of them. It doesn't matter what the doctor's report says. God can heal any disease that might come against you, and He will provide all you need to take possession of what He has promised.

The Body of Christ—men and women who love the Lord and are born of His Spirit—must choose to live by God's principles and promises. That doesn't mean we become professional religious students. We cannot be content to stay in training for the rest of our lives. God needs some surgeons—people who won't faint when Satan's victims are wheeled into the emergency room of the Spirit. God needs people who choose to use the tools He has given them—people who won't panic when the crisis comes. These are people who don't need to ask, "What page of the Bible should I turn to?" While their neighbors stand wondering, they are pulling their spiritual weapons off the shelf and using them!

You can only go as far as your choices will take you. If you choose to remain a slave, you will remain a slave. If you choose to stay on second base, you will stay on second base. If you choose to live a life of spiritual maintenance, you'll do it. But you can just as easily choose to rise up and scatter your enemies. You can choose to possess what God's promise says is rightfully yours.

God won't choose for you. He cannot force you to possess the land any more than He could force Moses's generation to possess theirs. He wanted much more for them than death in the desert. But He could not violate their free will. He would not force them to receive His best, and He won't force you. In the end, you will choose what you possess.

AFTER CROSSING THE JORDAN

The Scriptures reveal several keys to Israel's possessing the land after they safely crossed the Jordan. Joshua led them in three significant acts: they gave thanks to God, the men were circumcised, and the people celebrated the Passover.

They Gave Thanks

The first thing the Israelites did after crossing the Jordan was to build a memorial, a permanent testimony to the miracle God performed (Joshua 4:4-8). Joshua selected one man from each of Israel's twelve tribes to gather a stone and carry it to the other side as they crossed the riverbed. There, they set up camp and erected a memorial of twelve stones as an act of thanksgiving to God and a reminder for them and future generations that, without Him, the Israelites were nothing.

The memorial was also a fortress against pride. Thankful people dwell not on the greatness of self but on the greatness of God. They remember and are continually humbled and encouraged by their memories of God's mercy toward them. Israel still had many battles ahead and would need these reminders. Their faith had wavered in the past and would waver again. They were known to murmur, complain, moan, and groan as though their pitifulness would move God's hand. But God never inhabits His people's pitifulness. He inhabits their praises (Psalm 22:3).

Are you facing a battle? Remind yourself of past victories and praise God! Then, thank Him for His salvation in the present. In essence, you are erecting a memorial to His faithfulness that will glorify Him, get your mind off yourself, and stir your faith for what is ahead.

The Men Were Circumcised

The Israelites' miraculous crossing of the Jordan sent shockwaves through the land. The kings of the Amorites and Canaanites were terrified by what God did for His people, and they worried about what it meant for them. Meanwhile, God commanded that the sons of Israel be circumcised:

When all the kings of the Amorites who were on the west side of the Jordan, and all the kings of the Canaanites who were by the sea, heard that the LORD had dried up the waters of the Jordan from before the children of Israel until we had crossed over, that their heart melted; and there was no spirit in them any longer because of the children of Israel.
At that time the Lord said to Joshua, "Make flint knives for yourself, and circumcise the sons of Israel again the second time."

. . . So it was, when they had finished circumcising all the people, that they stayed in their places in the camp till they were healed. —Joshua 5:1-2, 8

While the local kings fretted over the power that Israel's God demonstrated, Joshua focused on the Lord's instructions and made certain that every man was circumcised. Under the New Covenant, the believer's heart is circumcised, but for the Israelites, the cutting away of the foreskin signified that they were God's covenant people. It was one of the reasons the giants of Canaan feared the Israelite warriors. The Canaanites understood that the Israelites' circumcision set them apart. It was the mark of their God, who had proven Himself mighty.

This mass circumcision not only marked God's people; it also marked a significant shift in their history. God Himself described the shift to Joshua:

So it was, when they had finished circumcising all the people, that they stayed in their places in the camp till they were healed. Then the LORD said to Joshua, "This day I have rolled away the reproach of Egypt from you." *Therefore the name of the place is called Gilgal to this day. —Joshua 5:8-9 (author emphasis)*

For born-again believers, Christ's sacrifice redeemed us and rolled away all reproach. Our hearts are to be continually circumcised and fixed on the One who keeps us and sets us apart. We are *His.*

They Celebrated the Passover

The third thing the children of Israel did after crossing the Jordan River was to celebrate the Passover. This was a special occasion: it was the first time they prepared the Passover meal from the produce of the Promised Land.

The Passover was another form of remembrance. But the feast's prophetic significance involved reconciliation and fellowship. It spoke of the power of the blood to cover sins (a subject we will discuss further in the next chapter), and it signified God's forgiveness and mercy, drawing His people deeper into fellowship with Him. The Passover also reminded Israel of God's supernatural protection when the death angel passed by their homes in Egypt, and not one of their firstborn sons died.

As the Israelites prepared for battle with the Promised Land's inhabitants, it was important for them to remember their testimony. In observing the Passover, they were saying, "God, we are Your people, and we are seeking You first. We know how much we need You. Help us to do Your will and be righteous before You."

We need God no less than Israel did. He has given us all of Himself, spilling not the blood of a lamb—but of the Lamb.

NEW LAND, NEW BLESSING

Once the children of Israel had built their memorial, circumcised their men, and celebrated the Passover, God confirmed His presence by blessing them. Scripture tells us that "the manna ceased on the day after they had eaten the produce of the land; and the children of Israel no longer had manna, but they ate the food of the land of Canaan that year" (Joshua 5:12).

Imagine if God had fed us with manna for four decades and suddenly stopped. We might not see that as a blessing but might think that God was withholding something. We would wonder, *Are we backslidden? Have we lost our place of fellowship with Him?*

In reality, the stopping of the manna revealed God's favor upon His people. He was not withdrawing His hand of blessing but leading them into new and greater blessings. The manna had served its purpose, and its cessation was a huge step forward in the fruitful land that God promised them. Instead of manna (which they complained about anyway), they would eat of the land's already legendary goodness.

This is an important truth. When you take possession of new territory, God might provide for you differently and perform different kinds of miracles. You don't need manna in a land that is flowing with milk and honey. That doesn't diminish God's former or future miracles. It simply reveals that you have entered a new place or season, and He has something more fitting in store.

Do you remember when God told Elijah to hide at the Brook Cherith in 1 Kings chapter 17? God had commanded ravens to feed Elijah there. Then, "it happened after a while that the brook dried up, because there had been no rain in the land" (1 Kings 17:7). Although his provision through the ravens (his "manna") had stopped, God had already prepared a new miracle for Elijah: He commanded a widow in Zarephath to feed him (1 Kings 17:9).

However, Elijah arrived at the widow's house during a drought. Except for a handful of flour and a little oil, her cupboard was bare. She was planning to use what little remained to make a final meal for herself and her son. Then, they would wait for starvation to run its course and end in death.

If we were in Elijah's shoes, we might have scratched our heads and wondered whether we heard God right or whether He had given us the wrong instructions. But God had a bigger miracle in mind than just feeding Elijah. He saw to it that everyone was fed, and the widow had an uninterrupted supply of flour and oil throughout the drought.

God always provides—but not always in the ways to which we are accustomed. When He leads us into new territory, He leads us into new miracles. I believe we are heading into new territory—yes, even in a time when chaos seems to be breaking out in every direction. The manna may have dried up, but God's provision for what is next will be no less miraculous than what He has done in the past. We might be leaving the old, but we are moving into the new. There might be some wonderful memories behind us, but we are moving toward even greater experiences. With God, nothing moves backward. He never directs us toward less but only toward more. He never beckons us downward but only leads us upward.

Keep in mind these keys to possessing the promise. Get them into your spirit and apply them to your life in every season. Get ready to savor the fruit of your new blessings, your inheritance. Get ready to enjoy the fatness of your promised land. Open your eyes to the goodness of your prophetic promise and expect God to keep His word. He is faithful!

THE KEYS BELONG TO YOU

What is your Jordan River? What will crossing it look like, and how will you memorialize what God has done?

Chapter 3

POWER OF THE BLOOD

You were not redeemed with corruptible things, like
silver or gold, from your aimless conduct received by
tradition from your fathers, but with the precious blood of
Christ, as of a lamb without blemish and without spot.
—1 Peter 1:18-19

When Israel celebrated the Passover at Gilgal, the land of their captivity was behind them, and the Promised Land was under their feet. But the lamb's blood still spoke of the God who covers His people and their sin. He had kept them throughout their wilderness journey. Now, He would keep them as they took the land He said was theirs.

The Passover foreshadowed the ultimate sacrifice of the Lamb of God, which is at the heart of the Christian faith. Tragically, much of the church has quit teaching about the blood that Jesus shed. Many preachers steer clear of the issue altogether, and fewer books are being written about it. In some quarters, the blood of Christ is being scrubbed from the Christian consciousness, leaving the tenets of the faith detached from its foundation.

I believe one reason for this stunning omission is vocabulary. Our violent culture attaches a negative connotation to the words *blood* and *bloodshed*. From a natural standpoint, it is understandable. The shedding of blood is horrific. So, the devil casts a shadow over the subject, even though he knows that the shedding of the Savior's blood has nothing to do with murder. For one thing, Jesus laid down His life (John 10:18). For another, His shed blood delivers us from death. Satan is clever, however. He uses our fear of violence to repel us from the powerful, central truth of Jesus's saving blood.

Scripturally, the sacrificial shedding of blood was the path to a reconciled relationship and the key to releasing God's favor and glory upon His people. In Christ's shed blood, God sees justification, the atonement, the remission of sins, reconciliation, the cleansing of our souls, the power to overcome, our place in the family of God, and the authority we have in Christ over the works of the devil. None of this would be available to us without Jesus's blood. We understand this by the revelation of our covenant relationship and position with Christ, both of which are established by His shed blood.

Unless we grasp the power of Jesus's blood and plead His blood over our lives, we will perpetually live beneath our birthright in God. We can blame this loss on the devil, but we are also to blame. In many Evangelical and Pentecostal circles, pleading the blood has lost its meaning, becoming a form of rhetoric that is divorced from revelation. We might be quick to say, "I plead the blood of the Lamb," but are we grasping the reality of Christ's sacrifice? Do we recognize all that His death and resurrection have afforded us?

This is not just a language problem but a revelation deficit that has contributed to our lack of power as a body. We don't need rhetorical expressions; we need to understand the dynamics involving the blood of the Lamb as revealed throughout God's Word. Without that, we cannot walk in the fullness of overcoming faith or of God's covenant promises.

WHY THE BLOOD?

Have you ever wondered why God chose blood as the path to reconciliation? Leviticus 17:11 has the answer: "The life of the flesh is in the blood, and I have given it to you upon the altar to make atonement for your souls; for it is the blood that makes atonement for the soul." As New Testament people, we focus on the precious blood of Christ. Inspired by the Holy Spirit, the apostle Peter explains why:

If you call on the Father, who without partiality judges according to each one's work, conduct your-selves throughout the time of your stay here in fear; knowing that you were not redeemed with corrupt-ible things, like silver or gold, from your aimless con-duct received by tradition from your fathers, but with the precious blood of Christ, as of a lamb without blemish and without spot. —1 Peter 1:17-19

God did not arrange our redemption through human stan-dards or religious traditions but by the blood of the Lamb, who is Christ Jesus. No other blood is as costly or valuable as His. Just as the natural blood brings life to the natural body, so the blood of Christ brings life to the covenant, and atonement cannot come apart from that life.

Just look at what the blood has done.

Jesus's blood paid the price for our redemption. Christ purchased man for Himself by spilling His own blood. Acts 20:28 says, "Therefore take heed to yourselves and to all the flock, among which the Holy Spirit has made you overseers, to shepherd the church of God which He purchased with His own blood."

Through His blood, Jesus Christ justified us. According to Paul, "God demonstrates His own love toward us, in that while we were still sinners, Christ died for us. Much more then, having now been justified by His blood, we shall be saved from wrath through Him" (Romans 5:8-9).

Jesus's blood brought us near to God. The only reason we sinful mortals can approach a holy God is because Christ's blood intervened on our behalf. Ephesians 2:12-13 reminds us that we:

Were without Christ, being aliens from the common-wealth of Israel and strangers from the covenants of promise, having no hope and without God in the world. But now in Christ Jesus [we] who once were far off have been brought near by the blood of Christ.

Jesus's blood makes atonement for our sins. In the Old Testament, atonement was a covering provided by the blood of animals to pacify or placate God's wrath. Animal blood could cover sin, but Jesus's blood broke sin's power. His blood "takes away the sin of the world!" (John 1:29)

The blood of Jesus restores. God's plan is to restore men and women to the estate from which they had fallen and bring them back to the place of power and authority they lost in the Garden of Eden. God would restore to them their true identity as people made in His image and likeness. Christ's sacrifice was complete and sufficient, "for by one offering He has perfected forever those who are being sanctified" (Hebrews 10:14).

Jesus's blood protects. The forms and rituals of religion offer no guarantee of protection. Our only hope is to stay within the covenants God has established with Jesus's blood. At the first Passover, God instructed the Israelites not only to sacrifice animals but also to apply their blood to the framework of the door and remain indoors overnight. Similarly, Christ's blood was shed, but we must consciously apply it to the doorposts and lintel of our hearts. Then, the enemy can rant, rave, and accuse all he wants, but he cannot come in. The blood protects us.

The blood of Jesus speaks. After Cain had killed Abel, the Lord told Cain, "The voice of your brother's blood cries out to Me from the ground" (Genesis 4:10). Christ's blood also speaks. It is "the blood of sprinkling that speaks better things" than the blood of Abel (Hebrews 12:24). Abel's blood was shed because of hatred, jealousy, and murder, and it cried out for vengeance and judgment. However, the blood that flowed from Jesus Christ did not call for vengeance or judgment. His blood cried out for the Father to show the world mercy and bring forgiveness, salvation, and redemption to the people. It spoke of something better.

The blood of Jesus is *powerful.*

God's plan is to restore men and women to the estate from which they had fallen and bring them back to the place of power and authority they had lost in the Garden of Eden.

THE BLOOD OF THE NEW COVENANT

God's new covenant with His people was sealed in His Son's blood. On the night He was betrayed, Jesus shared the emblems of the New Covenant with His closest disciples. He let them know that the New Covenant would rest upon His blood. After breaking the bread and eating it with them, "He also took the cup . . . saying, 'This cup is the new covenant in My blood, which is shed for you'" (Luke 22:20).

Christ's blood makes the New Covenant available to all who believe. It is the New Covenant in His blood. Without His blood, we cannot access the covenant or its benefits. Just as our physical blood carries oxygen to our organs and cells, the blood of the covenant carries the food of the Word. As we eat the Word, all that we need for life in Christ is imparted to us.

That same blood also cleanses us. Just as the red blood cells in our bodies carry carbon dioxide to our lungs to be exhaled, the blood of the covenant separates that which nourishes us from that which needs to be removed as waste. As the blood brings conviction for sin, rebellion, and wrath, it removes our "debris" and cleanses us: "If we walk in the light as He is in the light, we have fellowship with one another, and the blood of Jesus Christ, His Son, cleanses us from all sin" (1 John 1:7) and "To Him who loved us and washed us from our sins in His own blood" (Revelation 1:5).

The enemy's strategy is to contaminate our lives and introduce patterns that are neither clean nor righteous. His endgame is to destroy the essence of who we were invited to become in God. But just as the white blood cells in the physical bloodstream multiply themselves to fight off infections, so the power of God's Holy Spirit rises within us to fight off the enemy. Isaiah 59:19 says it this way: "So shall they fear the name of the LORD from the west, and His glory from the rising of the sun; when the enemy comes in like a flood, the Spirit of the LORD will lift up a standard against him." This verse is potent! I particularly like the way many rabbis render it: "When the enemy shall come in, like a flood the Spirit of the Lord shall lift up a standard against him." This reading (with the comma moved) reveals the Lord as the flood that rises up and overtakes the enemy.

Our God is a keeping God. Therefore, if we are sincere Christians, we find it hard to sin the way we once did. That doesn't make us sin-free people, but we do find it hard to sin freely. For one thing, the desire to sin is reduced when we follow Him faithfully. And when we do sin, the conviction of the Holy Spirit keeps our sin from taking root. Even if we try to deny our sin, we can't hide it from God. He knows us better than we know ourselves. When His Spirit convicts us, however, we have to respond to His conviction. He is not trying to hurt or embarrass us; He wants to stop the infections that invade our souls before they can destroy us.

We don't always repent immediately. When the prodigal son became spiritually ill, he told his father, "Give me the portion of goods that falls to me" (Luke 15:12). He wanted his inheritance but was unwilling to wait until after his father died. When his father agreed to his demand, he took off with the money and spent it all in "riotous living" (Luke 15:13, KJV). He persisted in his sin until it brought him to ruin and landed him in a pigpen. Yet, even there, God was present and fought for him.

If, like the prodigal, we stubbornly persist in having our own way, God can do little to help us. But leaving us in the pigpen can awaken us to the error of our ways. Because Christ's blood has been shed for us, the Holy Spirit won't give up on us, even when we have given up on ourselves.

Are you having a pigpen experience right now? God's Spirit is determined to convict you and bring you back to Father's house. He will not leave you—not even when you are neck-deep in muck. The pigpen was where the prodigal "came to himself" (Luke 15:17). The stubborn fellow who persisted in sinning finally repented and said, "I will arise and go to my father, and will say to him, 'Father, I have sinned against heaven and before you, and I am no longer worthy to be called your son. Make me like one of your hired servants'" (Luke 15:18-19).

Satan will try to corrupt your walk with all kinds of spiritual infections, but God has a purpose for your life. Once you enter into relationship with Him, He is committed to you and will not leave you defenseless. When something threatens your spiritual life, He "multiplies" His presence and attacks whatever threatens to harm you. Your part is to humbly plead the blood of Christ and look to Calvary. When you do, the Spirit of God will diagnose, attack, and destroy any infection. You don't have to understand how He does it. You just need to say, "God, I confess! I'm sick. Please help me."

OVERCOMING BY THE BLOOD

When you turn to God, keep your eyes on the cross, and plead the blood of Jesus, you will notice that certain battles with old temptations become easier to win. As you overcome in those areas, your testimony will help others and make you more effective in ministering to those who are struggling. You may have needed to separate yourself from them for a season, but there comes a point when being around people who are still spiritually sick does not endanger or tempt you as it once did. You can pray and talk with them without any fear of becoming infected.

This is not a psychological victory. Nor is it about your strength. It is a matter of applying the blood of Jesus to your heart and life. You will become able to deal with things that used to cause you trouble, and you will resist what you could not resist before. When you get delivered from the things that once drove you to the pigpen, you will be ready to help others.

We all face battles. Even the original apostles faced them. The Scriptures mention a battle the apostle Paul was in. There is no real explanation of what his torment was, but we know that he prayed three times for God to lift it. God's answer was perhaps unexpected—yet powerful. In 2 Corinthians 12:9, God said, "My grace is sufficient for you, for My strength is made perfect in weakness." Paul embraced God's response and said, "Therefore most gladly I will rather boast in my infirmities, that the power of Christ may rest upon me."

Paul understood the power of Christ that is manifested in His blood. That same power covers you. God wants to do for you that which you cannot do for yourself. Apply the blood of the Lamb, and let His grace be released in your life. God wants to build up your spiritual immune system until *nothing* can infect you.

When you get delivered from the things that once drove you to the pigpen, you will be ready to help others.

BLOOD, TESTIMONY, AND COVENANT

When dealing with the sin nature, there are no shortcuts. You cannot cast it out or rebuke it. Only the blood of Christ can conquer it. As long as you live in your earthly body, you will be tempted to sin. However, God did not leave you to contend with your temptation alone. Christ's blood has been shed for you. It not only cleanses you, but it speaks, just as it spoke to the death angel on the night of the first Passover. The blood on the lintels of your heart says, "Don't stop here. Just pass over and enter the doors where no blood has been applied."

You have a testimony. God has done great things for you through Jesus's blood. Greatest of all is how He washed you with His blood and purchased you with it. Therefore, the enemy can no longer treat you like his puppet. The apostle John said it this way:

> *Then I heard a loud voice saying in heaven, "Now salvation, and strength, and the kingdom of our God, and the power of His Christ have come, for the accuser of our brethren, who accused them before our God day and night, has been cast down. And they*

overcame him by the blood of the Lamb and by the word of their testimony, and they did not love their lives to the death." —Revelation 12:10-11

"The word of [our] testimony" and "the blood of the Lamb" are intertwined. The "word of [our] testimony" includes all the elements of our covenant with God, which was ratified by the shedding of Christ's blood. As blood-bought believers, both the Old and New Testaments are ours to claim. Without the Old Testament, we could not know exactly who Jesus is, particularly in relation to being the Messiah. Without the New Testament, we would not know that He fulfilled the promises God made under the Old Covenant. Both testaments are vital.

When we receive Jesus as our Lord and Savior, we become part of Christ's body, heirs of God who are counted as the offspring or seed of Abraham. We are not under the law but under Christ's blood. In the words of Paul, as inspired by the Holy Spirit, "*It is* of faith that *it might* be according to grace, so that the promise might be sure to all the seed, not only to those who are of the law, but also to those who are of the faith of Abraham, who is the father of us all" (Romans 4:16).

But what is Christ's body without His blood? If His blood does not flow through us, we are nothing, and we can do nothing. We are overcomers only by the blood of the Lamb and the word of our testimony. Then, God says, "When I see the blood, I will pass over you" (Exodus 12:13). Think of how our blood flows throughout our bodies and impacts every cell and organ. Well, Christ's blood flows to all parts of His body, of which we are a part. Therefore, His blood touches every area of our need. It feeds, cleanses, and protects us, doing for us things that we cannot do for ourselves.

You might think God is concerned only with so-called spiritual matters—how often you read your Bible, how frequently you pray, or how much you give to the church. But God looks at the totality of who you are. He is concerned for your entire being, and His blood is vital to every part of you. It reaches your job, family, relationships, state of mind, finances, and even your tastes and preferences. Nothing is left untouched by the blood of Jesus. Much the way the plasma carries blood throughout your physical body, so the blood of Jesus flows in and around and through you, feeding and washing each part of you and drawing you deeper into Him.

The blood also covers your physical healing. The Scriptures say that "He *was* wounded for our transgressions, He *was* bruised for our iniquities; the chastisement for our peace *was* upon Him, and by His stripes we are healed" (Isaiah 53:5). These "stripes" were the marks left behind by the cruel whip that lashed the Savior's back. His blood was shed through those stripes, and that blood brings healing to your physical body.

The blood of Jesus also covers your relationships and brings healing to them. It should be obvious that none of us can come into right relationship with others unless we are in right relationship with God. And we cannot be in right relationship with Him unless we are reconciled to Him by Jesus's blood. As Ephesians 2:13 says, "Now in Christ Jesus you who once were far off have been brought near by the blood of Christ."

We are "brought near" because the blood of Christ protects us from Satan's power. Satan comes "to steal, and to kill, and to destroy" (John 10:10). He is after more than our physical health and relationships. He is also out to destroy our mental health and emotional well-being. When depression or anxiety or fear or anything else that is not of God comes against us, we have two alternatives: (1) we can give in to our emotions, live under a dark cloud, and try to survive or (2) we can plead the blood of Jesus over the situation and emotions and gain victory over them.

God promised: "When I see the blood, I will pass over you; and the plague shall not be on you to destroy *you*" (Exodus 12:13). When the enemy comes against you emotionally or psychologically, remember what God promised. Then, say, "I plead the blood of the Lamb." When you do, you send that blood into every area of your thoughts and emotions, and God raises up a standard against the enemy.

This is not the power of positive thinking or any other discipline or mental therapy. It is the outworking of what you understand about God and His covenant with you. You understand that your hedge, shield, protection, and covering are not in what you have done or can do. By faith, you understand that the precious blood of Christ covers every aspect of your life, bringing His protection, covering, and very life to you.

Thank God for the blood of Jesus!

THE BLOOD FROM ANCIENT TIMES 'TIL NOW

Blood has played a part in the plan of redemption since the fall of man. After Adam and Eve sinned, God clothed them with the skins of animals slain for their redemption. Their blood was shed to appease the wrath of God and to bring Adam and Eve into a reconciled relationship with Him.

This blood-based relationship was not just for Adam and Eve. It was for their children and grandchildren and all succeeding generations. The Old Testament sacrificial system of the Hebrews was never about the flesh of animals but about their blood. When the meat of certain sacrifices was burned and offered up to God, the aroma that arose from that burning memorialized the blood that had been shed.

Circumcision also involved the shedding of blood. It was a token of the covenant being renewed for each descendant of Abraham. Every man who was circumcised, in essence, said, "Our family renews the covenant that was established between God and our Father, Abraham." God has determined that in New Testament times, it is the heart that is circumcised. Romans 2:29 says that the circumcision of the heart is done in the Spirit and not in the letter of the law, making us Jews inwardly.

As followers of Christ, we find symbols of our covenant in the communion service. Communion is a holy sacrament during which we symbolically partake of the sacrifice that established the covenant. Every time we take the elements, we publicly acknowledge the covenant, thereby renewing it. Each time, we are to fight the scavengers that would attempt to eat our sacrifice, and we are to examine our hearts, lest we be found to partake of the communion in an unworthy manner (Genesis 15:11; 1 Corinthians 11:27-29).

ESTABLISHED BY THE BLOOD

Our position with God is not established by our thoughts or feelings; it is established by the blood. Those moments when we don't feel particularly close to God do not change our position with Him. He has done what He said He would do. Our positional relationship is affirmed only by the power of Christ's shed blood. Our natural actions, religious works, and feelings cannot augment, diminish, or nullify that power.

The Scriptures are packed with promises, and anyone is free to read them. But only those who are covered with the blood of Christ can claim the promises of God and appropriate them for their daily lives. God is not obligated to release the contents of the Book to everyone. The Bible is powerful, but without the blood, we have no right to access the promises the Book contains.

At some point, the blood of Jesus must penetrate your spirit. That means the door of your spirit must open so that true communion can occur. Only then will Jesus sup with you, and you with Him. This communion takes place when you have properly discerned Christ's body and blood and have a genuine revelation of them. Going through the motions of the communion service will do nothing for you. But true communion is possible when you apply the blood of Jesus to your heart.

The blood is also essential to spiritual warfare. The only way to overcome the enemy is through the blood, which is the key to spiritual authority. Fasting and prayer are important. Your spiritual weapons are important. Perfected praise is important. But none of these are the most important. To overcome your enemy, the blood of the Lamb is most important. Without it, everything else is insufficient.

Some of us hope to gain victory through other people's faith. Some even travel long distances to receive the laying on of hands by the great ministers of our day. That is all well and good, but you will never have a complete victory through someone else's prayers. You might become better positioned to receive, and you might feel better after receiving the prayers and ministry of others. But you will never have an overcoming walk with God until you have properly applied the blood to your life. You must eventually come to the sure knowledge that Christ's blood was shed for you. The blood accesses the Book. The Scriptures and all the promises, which are true, can and will be yours as you become aligned to Christ through His sacrifice.

WE MUST DECIDE

For victory to be ours, we have to make some decisions: Either the blood of Christ has the power the Word of God describes, or it doesn't. Either it can protect us, or it can't. Either the Word of the Lord is true, or it isn't. We need to consciously decide and be aware of where we stand with these choices. The right decision or the wrong one will make all the difference.

If you have been born again, you have been "bought with a price" and are no longer your own (1 Corinthians 6:20, KJV). The same is true for me. My flesh is no longer *my* flesh, and my body is no longer *my* body. I belong to God, and in that regard, He has some responsibilities. One of them is to protect me from the enemy who is always looking for someone to devour.

God has given me Jesus's blood as my shield. The devil can come looking for trouble, but I am not an entrée for him. He is not free to devour me. My body, mind, soul, and spirit belong to God. God's Spirit bears witness with my spirit that I am His child (Romans 8:16). Hebrews 6:18 says that "it *is* impossible for God to lie." If He says the blood is my protection from the enemy and my freedom from the bondage of sin, then it is! The circumstances of my life might not always be ideal. Some problems might not be fully resolved. Yet, I can walk in hope and in freedom from bondage because of the blood that Jesus shed on Calvary for me.

May today be our day of decision. Let's accept these truths by faith, like little children who completely trust their loving Father. Let's also remember our part, knowing that the blood becomes effectual as we apply it, each to his or her own spirit. That is when change happens. That is when we realize that our Protector is standing between us and our enemy. So, let us silence the accuser and live victoriously, laying hold of the revelation of Jesus's blood. The enemy might try to destroy us, but when God sees the blood, He will prevent our foes from striking us down.

THE BLOOD APPLIED

In what specific ways has the blood of Jesus restored you to your rightful estate in the plan of God? How does that restoration form your way of life?

Part 2

EMPOWERED

for

THE PROMISE

Chapter 4

POWER OF THE DREAM

Now Joseph had a dream, and he told it to his brothers; and they hated him even more.
—Genesis 37:5

There is power in a dream. But it can only become a reality when the dreamer has the practical skills and spiritual virtues that lead to success. You can probably think of many people with dreams they long to fulfill. Some may find a measure of success, but only those who learn to balance their dreams, skills, and character will become like the great biblical dreamer, Joseph. With his brilliance, virtue, and uncompromised holiness, he honored the dreams God gave him. Joseph became the type of truly anointed person we should aspire to be.

Joseph was a rare individual. Few have prophesied as he prophesied or been supernaturally promoted and favored the way he was. And not many have learned to seize the moment like he did. As anointed human beings go, Joseph was a proto-type. Yet, he was not sinless. He was born of corruptible seed and made his share of mistakes. What set him apart from most people is what he learned about yielding to God. He loved God and fully surrendered to Him, despite the hardships he suffered. And he lived to reap the benefits of his surrender, not only for himself but for nations: "The LORD made all he did to prosper in his hand" (Genesis 39:3).

For us, Joseph epitomizes the empowered lifestyle. I am convinced that his prophetic and visionary giftings and his unique administrative talents were part of an anointing he began receiving very early in life. That anointing led Joseph to live differently from his brothers. He lived godly, which proved critical to the fulfillment of God's plan for him.

Joseph and his dream were vigorously tested. When his first dream foretold a great prophetic promise, he could have become prideful before God. But he remained humble and willing to serve. When he was despised by his brothers, misunderstood by his father, sold into slavery, lied against, betrayed, and imprisoned because he would not sin with an influential Egyptian woman, Joseph held fast to his relationship with God. Very early in life, he learned to value God's touch above all else, and he protected it at all costs.

Whether he was in the prison or the palace, Joseph maintained the attributes of someone who was guided and empowered in all things by God's Spirit. Although he had been wronged in many ways by many people, he did not smother his anointing with self-pity. Joseph diligently kept himself, year after year. When the path seemed chaotic, he kept his eyes straight ahead and carried himself like a man preparing for a destiny no one else envisioned. This posture would serve him well. No one could imagine what lay ahead for him, but as his dream began to manifest, Joseph would rise to the occasion.

Joseph lived his entire life as a testimony to God's power. In this and coming chapters, we will explore aspects of his life, beginning with his dreams. There is so much to learn from how he handled himself and the situations he faced. As you read, imagine yourself in Joseph's shoes, and allow the Holy Spirit to highlight any insights that will help you fulfill your destiny in God.

Whether Joseph was in the prison or the palace, he maintained the attributes of someone who was guided and empowered in all things by God's Spirit.

JOSEPH WAS DIFFERENT

Prior to Genesis 37, all that the Bible recorded of Joseph was that he was the son of Rachel. The very first account describing Joseph's life demonstrates the touch of God that was upon him:

> *Joseph, being seventeen years old, was feeding the flock with his brothers. And the lad was with the sons of Bilhah and the sons of Zilpah, his father's wives; and Joseph brought a bad report of them to his father. —Genesis 37:2*

Joseph was not your typical young man. He abhorred sin and could not turn a blind eye to it. When he saw his brothers involved in wrongdoing, it repelled him. Instead of joining in, as many younger brothers would have done, he told his father about it. Joseph wanted to see matters set right. It is easy to see why Jacob loved him so much. Joseph was an obedient and respectful son, and these traits were evident in everything he did. Just as Abraham had become aware that God's promises to him would come through Isaac, Jacob became aware early in Joseph's life that God's promises to him (Jacob) would come through this special son.

There was a problem, however: Jacob's favoritism infuriated his other sons and became a stumbling block for them. They saw Joseph as an irritant and became increasingly enraged by him. They resented how different he was from them. He would not imitate their bad behavior or act like an impressionable or rebellious youth. Instead, he carried himself like a prince, a young man of purpose who recognized a mission and holy calling on his life.

Joseph knew that his older brothers despised him. He may have discerned it even as a small boy and realized that he would pay a price within his family and community for the stand he took. But Joseph could not do otherwise. When sin was present, he blurted out the truth—not through weakness or a slip of the tongue but because he could not keep silent. Having taken his share of pushback from his older brothers, Joseph understood that his truth-telling had consequences.

THE POWER OF HERITAGE

Everyone knew that "Israel loved Joseph more than all his children, because he was the son of his old age" (Genesis 37:3). If that were not enough to rile Jacob's other sons, this was: "Also he made [Joseph] a tunic of *many* colors" (Genesis 37:3). Genesis 37:4 says that "when his brothers saw that their father loved him more than all his brothers, they hated him and could not speak peaceably to him."

In ancient times, men of power or royalty signified their choice of an heir with gifts. Jacob knew he would one day pass from the scene. Having so many sons, he would have to choose one to succeed him as head of the family and, therefore, head of the nation. The coat of many colors made his choice very plain.

Jacob had affection for Joseph, but the choice of his successor was not centered on his affections. It was God's choice to make, and God favored Joseph. Jacob simply responded to what everyone who knew Joseph could already see. But because Joseph's brothers were jealous of his anointing, they refused to acknowledge God's favor upon him and focused instead on expressing their displeasure.

Jacob knew better than to overlook God's preference. Because of his own history with God, Jacob understood destiny. God had once raised him up to be a divinely empowered prince. Now, as a seasoned patriarch, he saw in Joseph the qualities of character and integrity befitting an heir. Jacob based his choice on the visible evidence of God's blessing on Joseph's life. The coat visually acknowledged that blessing and Joseph's heritage and place in God's plan for Israel. People didn't wonder why Joseph was so colorfully adorned. They didn't say, "Look at that rebellious teenager!" They said, "Look! There goes the prince, the heir of Jacob."

Jacob's giving of the coat was a prophetic act. It declared to everyone that Joseph would be a man of authority. His brothers were not jealous that he had a better coat than they did. They all had good coats. They were a blessed family. What they envied was what Joseph would inherit—the leadership of the family and the nation. Having been rejected for that role, they begrudged God's choice and coveted everything Joseph would rightly receive.

Satisfied with God's choice, Jacob did not refrain from giving the coat to Joseph. Likewise, Joseph never downplayed the coat or questioned his father's gift. It never occurred to him not to wear it, or if it did, he wore the coat anyway. His brothers' choice to be offended was not his concern. He was empowered with a heritage that would release him into his destiny. In the end, even his brothers would understand and appreciate what God was doing.

Joseph's story is powerful in and of itself. Perhaps its greater power lies in its application to our lives. When you know you are an heir of God, you recognize the preordained blessing that awaits you. To possess it, however, you must allow God to mature you. Galatians 4:1 says that "the heir, as long as he is a child, does not differ at all from a slave, though he is master of all."

The revelation that God esteems you so highly as to make you His heir can release in you the confidence to achieve the dreams He gives you, whether they involve ministry, business, or family. It is then up to you to take the revelation to heart, guard it, and confidently wear your coat of many colors.

JOSEPH'S FIRST DREAM

Joseph's brothers hated him before he had his first dream. Yet he candidly shared it with them. Their response probably came as no surprise to him.

He said to them:

> *"Please hear this dream which I have dreamed: There we were, binding sheaves in the field. Then behold, my sheaf arose and also stood upright; and indeed your sheaves stood all around and bowed down to my sheaf."*
>
> *And his brothers said to him, "Shall you indeed reign over us? Or shall you indeed have dominion over us?" So they hated him even more for his dreams and for his words. —Genesis 37:6-8*

The brothers' relationships with Joseph had long been strained for all the reasons already mentioned. But when Joseph shared his first dream, their animosity worsened. Suddenly, their teenage brother demonstrated power as a visionary able to foretell the future.

This brought the simmering family conflict to a boil. It was about more than an annoying younger brother with a fancy coat. The brothers now saw in him a prophet, and it was almost more than they could bear. Livid, they called him "that dreamer." Joseph might have handled the situation with more tact, but in his youthful exuberance, he described exactly what God showed him. He almost certainly suspected his brothers' displeasure in advance but perhaps underestimated how offended they would be and, therefore, did not calibrate his presentation.

Joseph only knew that God had revealed something important, and he shared all of it. His naivete can be forgiven him. He was never one to pull back from the call of God, and he could not be expected to understand those who did. Light and darkness have nothing in common. Nevertheless, Joseph's delivery had consequences. His brothers' bitterness turned to a seething, lingering rage. It would take years for Joseph and his family to be reconciled.

There is a lesson evident in Joseph's story, one you may have already learned: people who are willing to pay a price for their anointing will be misunderstood. Those who are unwilling to pay such a price cannot or will not understand those who are. They misread people like Joseph and project their own insecurities on them. They accuse the Joseph types of being prideful, arrogant, or self-exalting. Yet, on the day of their calamity, they will travel great distances to find someone similarly anointed to pray for them!

Joseph's brothers were so enslaved by their emotions that they persecuted the brother whom God had chosen to "preserve life" (Genesis 45:5). Little did they know that their brother's "annoying" anointing would become a blessing to them and would save their families. In due time, they would appreciate the greatness for which God was preparing their brother.

JOSEPH KEEPS DREAMING

Regardless of how Joseph and his dream were received, he remained excited by what God revealed, and he stewarded the vision. He did not allow his loved ones' cruelty to smother it or his future authority. Yet, when we read the story, we need to put ourselves in his shoes and imagine what he was up against. Although he remained positive, the pressure of his brothers' persecution must have been daunting.

Amazingly, Joseph did not shrink back. It never occurred to him to quit dreaming or sharing his dreams just to keep the peace. I believe that because Joseph did the right thing with the first dream, God gave him a second dream, which caused even his father to rebuke him:

> *Then he dreamed still another dream and told it to his brothers, and said, "Look, I have dreamed another dream. And this time, the sun, the moon, and the eleven stars bowed down to me."*
>
> *So he told it to his father and his brothers; and his father rebuked him and said to him, "What is this dream that you have dreamed? Shall your mother and I and your brothers indeed come to bow down to the earth before you?" And his brothers envied him, but his father kept the matter in mind.*
> —Genesis 37:9-11

Joseph was now a man of prophetic dreams. His anointing was not for just a moment. It was threaded through his everyday life. He was flowing in a special prophetic gift of dreams and interpretation, which would cause him great pain but would one day lift him into greatness. He would not let the gift die in its incubation period just because his brothers failed to appreciate it. He nurtured God's plan and flatly refused to allow any portion of it to be aborted.

Joseph's most stalwart supporter was his father, Jacob. But Joseph's second dream confused even Jacob. He could not imagine that he and his wife would one day bow before Joseph, as the dream indicated. In the cultural climate of his day, parents did not bow to their children. So, Jacob rebuked Joseph for thinking such a thing. But he also recognized the anointing upon Joseph's life and kept the dream in mind. In other words, he pondered the matter and kept an open heart to see what would develop. Although tradition demanded that he put his son in his place, something about what Joseph said caused Jacob to stop short of outright rejecting it.

Often, the things that God declares to us in the Spirit seem nonsensical, in part because only He can know the end from the beginning. He is the only one who knows what future circumstances will prevail and what needs will arise. Sometimes, what He says seems contrary to our traditions, history, or personal experiences. But God does not work in the realm of the ordinary; He works in the realm of the extraordinary, which is harder for us to fathom.

We need to approach what God tells us the way Joseph did: without flinching. Despite the opposition he faced from the people who were closest to him, he nurtured his dreams and allowed himself to become everything God intended.

DREAMS, RESISTANCE, AND EMPOWERMENT

Joseph's brothers mocked him as though his dreams were silly. Practically speaking, they were. In the first dream, all the brothers were working in the field together, binding bundles of grain, when Joseph's bundle came to life and stood erect. Then, the brothers' bundles came to life and bowed in respect to Joseph's bundle. Wheat bundles don't do those things, so the brothers were comfortable in their cynicism. When the second dream proved even more dramatic, with the sun, moon, and eleven stars bowing to Joseph, the brothers had had enough.

Set aside for a moment the fact that Joseph's dreams were divinely symbolic. If the brothers really thought his dreams were silly, why didn't they dismiss them and move on? The fact that they were outraged forces one conclusion, which I alluded to earlier: many other signs were pointing to the greatness in Joseph's future. The hand of God was heavily upon his life, and everyone knew it. Therefore, his brothers could not dismiss his "silly" dreams. And because they would not accept what could not be dismissed, they perceived Joseph as a threat. They believed that his dreams just might come true.

So, they decided they had to stop him. The spirit that turned the brothers against Joseph was the antichrist spirit that has always been at work in the world. It was the same spirit that tried to destroy Moses before he could come of age and lead the Israelites out of bondage. Working through Herod, the same spirit tried to kill the infant Jesus and prevent Him from fulfilling His mission to redeem the world from sin.

Satan knows exactly how to stir people to jealousy, anger, and even murder. He riled Jacob's sons to such a degree that they wanted to kill their own brother. It was only Reuben's intervention that prevented them from doing it. Perhaps Reuben had a pang of conscience and realized how terrible it would be for his father to lose the son he loved most. Reuben didn't understand why his father felt the way he did about Joseph, but he respected Jacob enough to try to save the boy somehow.

The brothers finally agreed to sell Joseph into slavery and tell Jacob that he was dead. As Joseph was carried in bonds to Egypt, it must have seemed as though his dreams had died. But God gave him those dreams, and they and their prophetic significance would not die. They would be vigorously tested, however. Through all the hardships Joseph suffered, God used his dreams to empower him.

I believe that, without a prophetic dream, an anointed, empowered lifestyle cannot develop. God has never stopped speaking to His people. He is the God who imparts vision and gives His people big dreams. May we walk in the kind of faith that Joseph had and see our dreams become reality. May we be as determined as he was to resist all intimidation and the opposition of those who resent our dreams. And may God make our dreams a blessing to them even as He blesses us.

DREAMS WORTH FIGHTING FOR

Joseph and the dreams that represented God's promise were vigorously tested. How has your dream been tested, and how have you protected the dream and the promise it represents?

Chapter 5

THE POWER
OF VIRTUE

As for me, You uphold me in my integrity,
and set me before Your face forever.
—Psalms 41:12

From beginning to end, Joseph was a man of virtue, a person of high moral standards and moral excellence. The same could not be said of his brothers, who would go to any lengths to have their way. Jacob knew God's voice, and he knew his sons' strengths and weaknesses. He realized that what God called him to do would not be accomplished through Reuben or Gad or the other brothers. Joseph was another story, however. Jacob knew that God's heart was set on Joseph, and Joseph's heart was set on God.

Jacob's older sons displayed certain traits for which their father had once been known. Earlier in his life, Jacob was known as a deceiver and manipulator. His wayward sons represented that version of him well, but Jacob was not pleased by their emulation. He was no longer that man. He had been changed by God's touch at Bethel and was renamed Israel. He was now a prince who had power with God.

To his father's delight, this is the version of Jacob that Joseph emulated. The spirit of Israel had been imparted to Joseph, and Jacob saw it. Israel planted a seed of greatness in this son, and it took root. Joseph lived with a pure heart, a sense of vision, and the anointing.

Joseph's example did not reform his brothers, however. They were not concerned with God's intent for their family. They were driven by their anger and desire to get ahead in life. They were out to conquer the world, even if it meant betraying their brother and breaking their father's heart. Ten of them were older than Joseph and should have known better. But being older did not mean that they were more mature.

JOSEPH'S VIRTUE SET HIM APART

Joseph's older brothers became increasingly hateful toward him. When Jacob made his special coat, the rift got deeper. Joseph's brothers felt slighted by their father and believed that Joseph had usurped what belonged to them.

The brothers completely misunderstood Joseph. They saw him as a talebearer and boaster. But that is not at all what the Bible describes. Joseph was not playing family politics by informing on his brothers. He wasn't trying to turn Jacob against them. Nor was he trying to make a name for himself or curry favor with his father. He simply had a sense of purpose and was indignant toward evil wherever it showed up. You could say about Joseph what the Bible says about Job: He "feared God and shunned evil" (Job 1:1). Joseph would not tolerate wickedness and certainly could not remain silent when it corrupted his own family. The anointing that was on his life would not allow it.

When the anointing of God is upon your life, your character becomes so strong that you cannot remain silent and ignore wrongdoing, even if everyone else does. Other people might seem unbothered by godless acts, but you cannot sit still for them. If you are truly anointed, there are places you cannot bear to visit and situations you cannot tolerate.

Joseph's virtue was not for show. He wasn't like those who are anointed on Sunday but immoral on Monday. Joseph was anointed in the field and in the house. He was anointed in the marketplace and within his family circle. His virtue went with him wherever he happened to go. He had chosen to live like God's anointed man, and that required him to live a certain way all the time.

Joseph loved his brothers, but he would rather suffer their wrath than compromise his integrity to win their love. Over the years, his brothers let him witness their immorality and dishonesty. It's no wonder they couldn't stand to have him around! He knew their secrets, and they knew he had nothing to hide.

Joseph's predicament was plain. He had ten older brothers who chose to live ungodly while he remained committed to the narrow path. He was outnumbered and potentially overpowered. In the short-term, it would have been easier to follow their lead. But he could not. He knew that God required better of him. He understood that fulfilling his destiny would mean going against the flow of the world's ways. He would not have the "luxury" of winking at sin or being less than honest. He could not be underhanded, undercut the truth, or even teach his brothers a lesson for their unkindness toward him. He could not make choices based on his own desires or advantage, no matter the situation. He would have to swim against the tide. It would be painful but necessary.

When his brothers sold him into slavery, Joseph did not fight their treachery, although he could have. He was no longer a child and could have lashed out and tried to defend himself. But he didn't. As a man of character, he returned good for evil and left all judgment with the Lord. He would not stoop to compromise even while he was being betrayed.

When we refuse to get down in the mud with the people who wrong us, steal from us, or try to destroy our good names, God gives back to us everything they took, and more. Joseph's life testifies to this truth. Neither Reuben's plan nor the plans of the other brothers accomplished what they intended. Instead of doing away with Joseph, their betrayal led to his elevation to high places and the saving of countless lives, including their own.

VIRTUE AND OBEDIENCE

Joseph's virtuous living was rooted in his obedience. The actions that irritated his brothers were not directed at them. They were done in submission to God. Because Joseph's brothers were blinded by hatred and envy, they misunderstood his motives and did not (or would not) recognize God's hand on him. It never occurred to them that God had anointed him for reasons that would become evident in the future and would involve their own survival.

Except for Benjamin, Joseph was the youngest of the brothers. Yet he was more clear-eyed than all of them. He understood that he was called to lead, and he honored his calling by obeying God. When his circumstances seemed to contradict what his dreams had revealed, Joseph did not second-guess God or quit obeying Him. When his brothers mistreated him, he turned the other cheek. When his father sent him to care for the brothers who never cared for him, he served them. When he was unjustly imprisoned, he was a model prisoner who served and helped others. And when Potiphar's wife attempted to seduce him, he removed himself from a situation that lesser men might have welcomed.

Joseph's sense of identity guided his choices and was formed around his dedication to God's principles and plan for his life. He knew that the powerful dreams God gave him would not be fulfilled unless he withstood adversity and maintained his integrity, regardless of the cost or his feelings. By living this way, Joseph kept himself pure and prepared for better things.

Please be aware that I am not deifying Joseph, and we should not deify him. I don't believe God allowed him to be one of the most prolific Bible characters so that we would idolize him. He was an impeccable role model, but he was not a superhero. He was a man—an anointed man who was birthed out of the common ground we all share called *imperfection*. He did not rise to greatness because he had superpowers. He simply lived a surrendered life that allowed God to work in and through him to achieve what He had ordained.

IMPASSIONED SPIRITUALITY AND PRACTICAL SKILLS

The fullness of Joseph's calling demanded excellent character, but it also required practical abilities. Joseph readied himself for his destiny by balancing the two. His impassioned spirituality made him zealous for God and intolerant of evil, and his practical skills convinced Pharaoh that he was indispensable to Egypt's survival.

Spiritual fire and practical genius are not opposite forces but complementary ones, as Joseph's life shows. His spiritual passion and desire to obey God fueled his practical genius and made him diligent in all things. Instead of allowing himself to rot in prison, Joseph kept his heart and mind clear and was ready to seize every opportunity when it arrived. He did not know what his breakthrough would look like or when it would come, but he was going to meet it head-on.

KNOW YOUR DEFENDER

Swimming against the current can get lonely. When those who are ruled by the money god, the pride god, or some other idols strive to gain every possible advantage, it can seem like the whole world is getting ahead of you.

In those moments when you wonder where your virtue is getting you, remember who has your back. Outside resistance is inevitable, but God "saves the upright in heart" (Psalms

7:10). He is your defense, and He is a promise keeper. So, stand on His promise from Psalms 32:10-11: "Many sorrows *shall* be to the wicked; but he who trusts in the LORD, mercy shall surround him. Be glad in the LORD and rejoice, you righteous; and shout for joy, all *you* upright in heart!" Even when you feel like you are losing ground, God's mercy surrounds you. He is working all things for your good (Romans 8:28).

Look at what Psalms 37:37 says: "Mark the blameless *man* . . . for the future of *that* man *is* peace" (Psalms 37:37). God is telling the whole world to make a mental note of the blameless. Watch what happens in their lives and emulate them. God is blessing them, just as He blessed Joseph. Even fresh from prison, God's blessing was on him. When Joseph interpreted Pharaoh's dreams, "Pharaoh said to his servants, 'Can we find *such a one* as this, a man in whom *is* the Spirit of God?'" (Genesis 41:38) Pharaoh recognized God's hand on Joseph and appointed him—a stranger and a Hebrew—to high office in Egypt! Joseph believed he was destined for greatness; now the most powerful ruler in the world affirmed his destiny.

Joseph's Defender had been working on his behalf all along. Joseph's brothers assumed that enslavement would destroy him. They thought they had snuffed out his dreams and removed him from their lives permanently. But they were wrong. God defended Joseph. In every dark place Joseph found himself, God was his light. He continued moving Joseph toward the blessing that made his brothers envy him in the first place. The pathway didn't look like what Joseph or anyone else would have expected. But he reached his destination all the same.

INTEGRITY WITH HUMILITY

No matter what the world and the devil threw at Joseph, he maintained his integrity. Proverbs 10:9 says, "He who walks with integrity walks securely, but he who perverts his ways will become known." The word translated *securely* means "confidently."[4] Joseph's integrity made him surefooted and able to navigate the difficulties he encountered on the way to his prophetic promise. He wasn't confused or directionless. His integrity kept him moving forward, even when his circumstances seemed to contradict his God-given dreams.

When you walk in integrity, you can walk like a champion because your prophetic perspective will give you supernatural clarity—even when your circumstances contradict everything God has said to you. I am not advocating a prideful or haughty attitude. Righteousness and pride don't mix. Joseph's confidence was not grounded in himself but in his relationship with God. He was confident but humble, knowing he was in God's hands. Being humble doesn't mean being bent over, downtrodden, and kicked aside like an old shoe. True humility means you recognize your dependence on God and are secure in it.

Proverbs 14:11 says, "The house of the wicked will be overthrown, but the tent of the upright will flourish." When you walk humbly, you can stop worrying about what will happen when you reject popular opinion and refuse to play worldly games. You can stop worrying about peer pressure and start responding to the Holy Spirit. Let God's voice become louder

---

4   Blue Letter Bible, s.v. "betah," accessed September 11, 2023, https://www.blueletterbible.org/lexicon/h983/nkjv/wlc/0-1/.

in your heart than it has ever been. Allow His voice to drown out the noise that is vying for your attention. Let Him convict you of anything in your life that is not pleasing to Him. Let Him uncover anything that is not Christlike. And let Him make you His prince or princess for all to see.

THE POWER OF HOLINESS

The life that Joseph cultivated was a life of holiness. Long before his meeting with Pharaoh, "Potiphar, an officer of Pharaoh, captain of the guard, an Egyptian, bought him from the Ishmaelites who had taken him down there" (Genesis 39:1). Potiphar recognized Joseph's excellence and saw God's mark on him. He developed so much trust in Joseph that he made him overseer of his house. From that point on, "the LORD blessed the Egyptian's house for Joseph's sake; and the blessing of the LORD was on all that he had in the house and in the field" (Genesis 39:5).

For the first time in years, people recognized Joseph's unique gifts and appreciated the touch of God that was upon his life. Since being in Egypt, he'd risen meteorically from the position of a simple slave to the overseer of an estate. Joseph's future looked bright. He had no way of contacting his family, but because of his dreams from God, he was confident that they would eventually hear about what God was doing in his life. He could not know how or when it would happen, but it *would* happen.

Then, something terrible happened: his master's wife attempted to seduce him. It might seem odd that a woman of high estate would consider such a risky relationship, but it's not necessarily unusual. The anointing makes you unique and brings out the special characteristics that make you attractive to other people. Those who are spiritual recognize that the Spirit of God is drawing them, but those who are of the world cannot accurately identify the attraction and may assume that it is physical.

Potiphar's wife couldn't help but notice that Joseph was unusually compassionate, understanding, and caring. He was sincere and honest and meant what he said. Potiphar's wife appreciated these qualities. She also appreciated the fact that "Joseph was handsome in form and appearance" (Genesis 39:6). Yet, he was also a slave who had nothing to offer a woman in high society. There had to be more to this risky move than mere physical attraction. I believe that deep down, Potiphar's wife desired to be identified with Joseph's spirit, and the only way she knew how to do that was through a physical relationship.

Potiphar's wife set in motion a dangerous turn of events. She deceived many, including her husband, and she complicated Joseph's already difficult situation. He was lonely, far from home, and perhaps flattered to know that a prominent woman was interested in his affections. Still, he was not about to sin against God. He could not accept her advances, even though resisting them would also cause him trouble.

Some men might have thought long and hard before angering a woman as prominent as Potiphar's wife. But not Joseph. He made the only choice he could make: he rejected her advances and told her exactly why:

"Look, my master does not know what is with me in the house, and he has committed all that he has to my hand. There is no one greater in this house than I, nor has he kept back anything from me but you, because you are his wife. How then can I do this great wickedness, and sin against God?" —Genesis 39:8-9

Joseph's holiness would not allow him to violate his master's trust or surrender to his attractive wife. Potiphar had been good to Joseph. The man may have been a pagan, but he recognized the Spirit of God when he saw it in Joseph. Joseph respected him far too much to betray him.

Joseph also valued God's blessing and empowerment more than he valued any gratification of the flesh. He was not about to jeopardize his inheritance. God had not sent him to Egypt to be consumed by a tryst. God sent him there to become Egypt's prime minister. Joseph was determined to keep himself pure and prepared for the day of his supreme service. So, in his own way, he told Potiphar's wife, "I can't do it."

Joseph walked in true holiness, which is the essence of God's nature. He embraced that nature and became a partaker of it (2 Peter 1:4). It was not a matter of refusing temptation in his own strength. It was about letting God do the work in him over time so that when the temptation came, only one answer came to Joseph's mind. It was not all about what Joseph *wouldn't* do. If he had removed every sinful thought and pattern from his life and not replaced them with God's love, he would not have been holy; he would have had a life full of holes. But Joseph had learned about God's love and how to walk in it. Holiness was part of his being.

Look at what Ephesians 4:23-24 says: "Be renewed in the spirit of your mind, and . . . put on the new man which was created according to God, in true righteousness and holiness." The phrase "true righteousness and holiness" indicates that counterfeits are possible. But there is no joy in them. True righteousness and holiness are a joy. When they are present, you know that you have missed nothing in life, sacrificed nothing, and yet gained everything in the process.

Maintaining an anointed, empowered lifestyle means embracing the call to be holy. It is not just for the preacher but for the businessperson, the blue-collar worker, and the professional as well. It is not just the husband and wife but also for the children. All of us are called to live holy, out in the open and behind closed doors.

You might experience a measure of success and fulfillment without virtue. Many godless people have accumulated wealth and fame. But wealth and fame will not satisfy you in this life or serve you in eternity. Only godly, virtuous people can succeed in God's calling and fulfill their destinies. Only they can partake of the life God ordained for them in love.

Charisma without character is dangerous!

THE COST AND CROWN OF VIRTUE

How does virtue set you apart? From what does it separate you, and to what (or whom) does it graciously bind you?

Chapter 6
POWER TO ENDURE

Blessed is the man who endures temptation; for when he has been approved, he will receive the crown of life which the Lord has promised to those who love Him.
—James 1:12

J ames chapter 1 is rich with insights about the practice and benefits of enduring. Obviously, the chapter was written long after Joseph's earthly life ended, yet Joseph lived as though he'd memorized the following passage and was determined to embody every word of it:

My brethren, count it all joy when you fall into various trials, knowing that the testing of your faith produces patience. But let patience have its perfect work, that you may be perfect and complete, lacking nothing. If any of you lacks wisdom, let him ask of God, who gives to all liberally and without reproach, and it will be given to him. But let him ask in faith, with no doubting, for he who doubts is like a wave of the sea driven and tossed by the wind. —James 1:2-6

And later: "Blessed *is* the man who endures temptation; for when he has been approved, he will receive the crown of life which the Lord has promised to those who love Him" (James 1:12).

Enduring is not about passively putting up with whatever comes your way. To endure is "to remain firm under suffering or misfortune without yielding."[5] That requires a proactive approach to life's challenges that keeps your heart fixed on completing God's will. For Joseph, it meant not pining about the unfairness of his situation but keeping his eyes on where God was leading him.

You could say that Joseph wrote the book on enduring. He never yielded to the pressures he faced but positioned himself to receive "the crown of life" (James 1:12). Every difficulty he faced increased his ability to endure, and that endurance lifted him above the schemes of the antichrist spirit that sought to deter him. Joseph became a master of enduring hardship and resisting self-pity. He wasn't consumed by either. He simply let "patience have *its* perfect work," and he became "perfect and complete, lacking nothing" (James 1:4).

Joseph was a virtuous man who developed endurance as a virtue all its own. He did not indulge in the self-focused human impulses that most people resort to in their suffering. Enduring was so important to Joseph that he reined in his emotions and remained "swift to hear, slow to speak, slow to wrath," even when he was pressed to the limit (James 1:19). Joseph knew that "the wrath of man" could "not produce the

---

5 *Merriam-Webster*, s.v. "endure," accessed September 20, 2023, https://www.merriam-webster.com/dictionary/endure.

righteousness of God" (James 1:20). So, he looked "into the perfect law of liberty and [continued] in it" (James 1:25).

By enduring, Joseph allowed himself to remain faithful to God's direction. He was "not a forgetful hearer but a doer of the work" who was "blessed in what he [did]" (James 1:25). That was Joseph's secret: he strove to do everything God asked of him, the way God asked him to do it, no matter how difficult it seemed. His endurance empowered him to rise to the heights of his calling, something few people of his young age (or any age) ever experience.

Joseph did not endure as a show of his own strength or for the sake of his own glory. He faithfully developed the power to endure for God's glory and the saving of many lives. He was committed to the divine plan and nothing else.

KEEPING AN OPEN HEART

To endure throughout his long journey, Joseph had to maintain a particular posture and perspective—a practiced openness to God's will and ways. He had to see his life and future, not through the lens of his own desires or preferences but through the lens of God's plan and purposes.

Joseph was clear about where his role ended and God's role began. He knew God's hand was on his life. And he knew that some people meant to harm him or prevent him from fulfilling his destiny. But those people were not his problem to solve; they were God's. Joseph never allowed them to hijack his attention. He looked only to God, believing and trusting Him to iron out all the crooked places and people in his life.

He was humble toward God and chose not to get ahead of Him just to protect himself.

This is a crucial lesson in learning to endure. People like Joseph understand that God always intervenes in one way or another to accomplish His will. They also know that He can use other people's desires—even the misguided ones—to get it done. Joseph's brothers were convinced that they could cut him out of the picture and have things their way. But God had something altogether different in mind. As far as He was concerned, all their scheming would serve His purposes and not theirs.

Yet having things God's way still required Joseph's endurance, even when it seemed to prolong his suffering. Rather than allowing his emotions to drive him, Joseph allowed God to lead him. He did not fight against his brothers or resist the Midianites who delivered him into slavery. He knew that God was with him, and he allowed God to lead him into his prophetic promise by way of a painful path. No matter what happened, Joseph kept following God. In the end, he was blessed, and God was glorified.

This is a powerful key to standing firm in your faith: when your circumstances worsen, don't panic! Even chaos can't change God or His plan. Long before you saw the crisis coming, God prepared your path forward, and He stocked it with every form of provision you would need to succeed. Just keep your heart open to His love, His power, and His ways. Remember that He is attentive to you and is with you. When necessary, He will shake other people awake, make them aware of your predicament, and cause them to pray or help you in some unexpected way. Just relax in the Lord's arms, and know that everything will be all right.

TRUST THE GOODNESS OF GOD'S INTENT

When life gets hard, the enemy always points a bony finger at God and accuses Him of letting you down. To be empowered to endure, you must remember that everything God intends for you is good. The devil will run his mouth, but anything he says is a lie. Yes, trouble might come and might even shake you for a time. But you are empowered to endure difficult seasons and overcome them—not in your own strength but because the omniscient, omnipotent, omnipresent God of the universe never leaves you or forsakes you (Hebrews 13:5).

"God *is* not a man, that He should lie" (Numbers 23:19). He doesn't break His promises or let His people down. He never changes. Even when He allows challenges to touch your life, He knows what He is doing. In everything that God allows, He has a higher purpose in mind. You can endure, knowing that the final outcome will be for your good. God is not in the business of putting His servants through hell on earth. He does, however, have a specific plan, and it sometimes requires circumstances you would not readily choose. But know this: when He delivers you from them, you will be positioned to apprehend your destiny.

Did you hear what I just said? The day is coming when you will look back on your current trials with gratitude. You will see that as you trusted God, He turned your trials into triumphs and your challenges into conquests for His kingdom. Years from now, people who know what happened will realize that you "should be dead," but you're alive; you "should be broke," but you are prospering; you "should be divorced," but your marriage is stronger than ever. They will have no choice but to glorify God for the anointing of His Spirit that sets you apart and keeps you.

As Christ's body, we have nothing to fear, even when it seems like a great conspiracy is working against us. We don't need to rescue ourselves or reason our way out of our trials. Instead, we can release our cares to God and let Him deal with them as only He can. He will intervene for us and keep us standing until the storm passes, but He will do it His way. He said, "Do not avenge yourselves, dear friends, but give place to God's wrath, for it is written, 'Vengeance is mine, I will repay,' says the Lord" (Romans 12:19, NET).

There is no gain in second-guessing God or doubting His methods. If Shadrach, Meshach, and Abed-Nego had questioned God's goodness, they would have shrunk back from the fire in the Babylonian furnace. Then, neither Nebuchadnezzar nor his people would have witnessed God's glory. Instead, when Nebuchadnezzar ordered the fire to be made seven times hotter, the three young Hebrews stood fast. They would not let Nebuchadnezzar bully them into compromising or doubting God. They were committed to the divine call and would do whatever it required of them. And what happened? Jesus met them in the fire, and the fire—the seven-times-hotter fire—could not hurt them! (See Daniel 3:24-25.)

Do you remember Jesus's words when He sent out a group of seventy disciples? He told them, "I send you out as lambs among wolves" (Luke 10:3). The idea wasn't an enticing one. But Jesus wasn't selling anything. He was simply letting the seventy know what they were up against. As intimidating as their prospects seemed, they trusted His intentions and went out among the "wolves." They soon returned with joy, saying, "Lord, even the demons are subject to us in Your name" (Luke 10:17).

Of course, Jesus wasn't surprised at the outcome. He knew exactly what would happen and said, "Behold, I give you the authority to trample on serpents and scorpions, and over all the power of the enemy, and nothing shall by any means hurt you" (Luke 10:19).

Like the three Hebrew boys and the seventy disciples, Joseph was faithful to God and trusted His intent. But Joseph was also human. I am sure that he wondered why certain things happened the way they did. Yet his wondering did not lead to wandering. Joseph pressed forward because he was sold out to God. He could have decided that being different from most people was not worth the trouble it caused him. He could have seen his separation unto God as being too high a price to pay. But he didn't. He accepted opposition as part of his calling. He trusted God and set himself in unshakable agreement with His intent. Having opened his heart and life to God, he was determined to complete his course. He kept his eye on the prize, even though it would elude him for many years to come.

ENDURING WHAT YOU DON'T UNDERSTAND

Much of what Joseph endured would have been hard to understand. Imagine being in his sandals when his brothers threw him into the pit and calmly ate and drank while he suffered from thirst, hunger, and the agony of their betrayal. Now, picture yourself suffering the humiliation of being carried off in bonds to a life of enslavement, knowing that your own brothers were willing to put you through hell. How could Joseph make sense of all that happened to him?

The short answer is that whether or not Joseph could explain the injustices he suffered as he suffered them, he had no choice but to endure them. He would surely have tried to understand his brothers' reasoning, and he probably wondered what other atrocities might be ahead. If I were in his predicament, I would certainly have rehearsed everything that led up to the moment of my betrayal and would have wondered why God permitted such a thing to happen. I can only imagine that Joseph also wondered why his situation looked so different from what his dreams had shown him. There, his brothers honored him, but now, they mocked him and sold him for money.

The brothers' actions would have so traumatized Joseph that merely surviving would require more strength than a human being could muster. But with God's help, Joseph survived. That tells me that he tapped into the strength that was beyond himself. I believe he rehearsed the promises of God, again . . . and again . . . and again, until he was able to stand firm whether he understood his situation or not. How else could Joseph have endured his brothers' cruelty? How else could he have coped with all that was thrust upon him?

Joseph's ability to endure was essential. He had a lot on his plate and was surrounded by uncertainty. He had no way of knowing when he would see his father again or if he would ever see him. Had he known from the start that their separation would last thirteen years, he would surely have been anxious. But he could not afford to let his mind wander. He had to filter all his anxious thoughts through the prism of everything God had already shown him about his future. God had not given him a picture of sorrow and destruction; He showed him a future of exaltation and greatness, and that is what Joseph had to remember.

EMBRACING DIVINE DELAYS

Does it seem that with every step forward, you take two steps back? We all know the feeling. Often, the sense of losing ground is based on our ideas about how things *should* go. But our conclusions are based on our limited view of the larger picture. We forget that some delays are divinely orchestrated for our benefit. When we keep this fact in mind, however, we can humbly seek God's perspective and cooperate with His timing.

The truth is that living an anointed, empowered lifestyle requires us to accept divine delays. Intellectually, we affirm that God's timing is perfect, but our human restlessness doesn't allow us to wait. We seem to fear delays, as though they were signs of failure, rejection, or God's negation of His own promises. But these generalizations paint the wrong picture. They mischaracterize God and the situation because they are based on a misunderstanding of His ways. When we reflect, reconsider, and remind ourselves that He's got our backs, we can more easily accept His schedule, and we will value our time in His "waiting room." Instead of being frustrated by it, we will learn to embrace it, realizing that it is a season of strategic preparation and positioning.

Joseph's years in God's waiting room were essential to his victory. One day, he was surrounded by his family and living in the assurance of God's glorious promises; the next day, he was stripped, bound, and carried off to Egypt. Not only did Joseph seem to be losing time, but he lost all freedom and security. Having long been sheltered in his father's favor, he was now exposed to all kinds of danger. He must have felt, at least at first, that he had lost ground—*lots of ground*! Yet, in his long season of waiting, Joseph learned things he could not have learned in the comfort of Jacob's house. And he made the adjustments that helped him not only to survive but to fulfill his destiny.

As far as Joseph's natural eyes could see, his dreams had evaporated. But his conduct throughout his ordeal suggests that the eyes of his heart saw something else. Strangely enough, the Bible says very little about his trip to Egypt with the Midianites. We can only imagine how excruciating it was, yet Scripture devotes only two sentences to that portion of Joseph's ordeal: "Then Midianite traders passed by; so *the brothers* pulled Joseph up and lifted him out of the pit, and sold him to the Ishmaelites for twenty *shekels* of silver. And they took Joseph to Egypt" (Genesis 37:28).

I believe so little was said because what Joseph suffered during the trip itself was not important in the light of eternity. God empowered Joseph to endure the shock, the poor treatment, the disorientation, and the sense that his life had been derailed. It wasn't that God lacked compassion for Joseph or was not present to him in his suffering. Quite the contrary! The fact that Joseph endured the trauma of his betrayal and the journey to Egypt is evidence that God was with him every step of the way.

Although Joseph's God-ordained future seemed lost, he excelled in Egypt and found great favor. As shocking as his separation from his family had been, he did not wallow in self-pity or in his suffering. Instead of becoming bitter over delays, he poured himself into whatever task was before him—as a slave in Potiphar's house, as a prisoner in Pharaoh's dungeon, and as an interpreter of dreams.

Joseph's years in Egypt looked like a delay arranged by the devil himself. But Joseph knew better and approached every apparent setback as an opportunity to prepare for the greatness that was still ahead. By valuing divine delays, he cooperated with God's unfolding of his promised destiny.

MAKING EVERY MOMENT COUNT

When Potiphar promoted Joseph and entrusted him with running his household, he acknowledged Joseph's excellence. Even as a man enslaved, Joseph made every moment in Potiphar's house count. If the life Joseph had been expecting was going to be delayed, he was determined to prosper while he waited.

Joseph's attitude was wise beyond his years. The time he spent serving Potiphar allowed Joseph, a stranger in a strange land, to build a reputation and a resumé—just by being himself. Genesis 39:2-3 says, "The LORD was with Joseph, and he was a successful man; and he was in the house of his master the Egyptian. And his master saw that the LORD *was* with him and that the Lord made all he did to prosper in his hand." Potiphar had a good thing in Joseph, and he knew it. Verse 5 adds, "The LORD blessed the Egyptian's house for Joseph's sake; and the blessing of the LORD was on all that he had in the house and in the field."

Joseph gained in favor because he continually proved himself to be an asset. Serving a man as wealthy and powerful as Potiphar was a golden opportunity to learn how to successfully administrate a large estate. This on-the-job training honed Joseph's skills and laid a foundation for his future success as overseer for the land of Egypt.

Amazingly, Joseph's "lost" season in Egypt accelerated his maturation as a leader. Had he remained at home, he would have continued in his father Jacob's favor and would have become the leader of the family when Jacob died. But in Potiphar's house, Joseph learned to handle great responsibility and authority long before his father passed away. God knew that Joseph needed this expedited training. It helped him to take charge at a moment's notice on the day Pharaoh called him out of the dungeon.

Of course, the ground that Joseph gained as Potiphar's overseer seemed to be lost when Potiphar's wife unjustly accused him of molesting her. But God preserved Joseph's gains in the long run. Even his imprisonment in the "place where [Pharaoh's] prisoners *were* confined" had a purpose (Genesis 39:20). Joseph knew better than to let another delay crush him. So, he treated his prison stay like one more opportunity to make every moment count. He chose to endure with a sense of purpose, serving others and sharpening his skills, which proved essential to his ultimate promotion. He was exactly where he needed to be, and he would eventually see why he needed to be there. In the meantime, he burnished his resumé:

> *The LORD was with Joseph and showed him mercy, and He gave him favor in the sight of the keeper of the prison. And the keeper of the prison committed to Joseph's hand all the prisoners who were in the prison; whatever they did there, it was his doing. The keeper of the prison did not look into anything that was under Joseph's authority, because the LORD was with him; and whatever he did, the LORD made it prosper. —Genesis 39:21-23*

Joseph could not help but prosper himself and the people he served, even as an inmate. Yet this was not the final divine delay that he would face on the road to his destiny. Another interruption was ahead, and this one involved the most powerful man in the world:

> *Pharaoh was angry with his two officers, the chief butler and the chief baker. So, he put them in custody in the house of the captain of the guard, in the prison, the place where Joseph was confined. And the captain of the guard charged Joseph with them, and*

he served them; so they were in custody for a while.
—Genesis 40:2-4

Pharaoh's chief butler and chief baker were high-profile prisoners, and the jailer put them in Joseph's care. The dungeon was not the kind of place anyone would choose to call home but something divine was afoot. Joseph's new charges presented an opportunity that he could not have arranged for himself.

On the surface, Joseph's job was to organize the prison's food service and cleaning crews. But God had much more in mind. In this place of obscurity, Joseph would establish a reputation as a man who could interpret dreams and other spiritual matters. The arrival of Pharaoh's butler and baker was not a random event. It was Joseph's chance to serve and to advance along his God-ordained path.

When "the butler and the baker . . . *were* confined in the prison, [they] had a dream, both of them, each man's dream in one night *and* each man's dream with its *own* interpretation" (Genesis 40:5). The next morning, Joseph visited the men in their cell and noticed that they were despondent. Because he had a servant's heart, he took an interest in those who were in his charge. So, he asked the men what the matter was. They told him, "We each have had a dream, and *there is* no interpreter of it" (Genesis 40:8).

The door had opened for Joseph, and he recognized it. He also understood the men's distress and offered to help them, saying, "Do not interpretations belong to God? Tell [the dreams] to me, please" (Genesis 40:8). Joseph's offer might have taken the men by surprise, but dreams and their interpretations were his specialty. He knew where his gift originated. He had been hearing from God since his childhood and was confident that He would reveal the meanings of the men's dreams now.

Of course, this would prove critical to the butler and baker because each man's dream was a matter of life and death. The butler's dream prophesied his release from prison and his return to Pharaoh's service. The baker was not so fortunate. His dream foretold his imminent execution. In both cases, however, Joseph maintained his integrity and gave the interpretations exactly as he received them. For better or worse, each man knew precisely what the Lord had revealed.

Joseph asked nothing of the men except for one favor from the butler. Joseph said to him:

"Remember me when it is well with you, and please show kindness to me; make mention of me to Pharaoh, and get me out of this house. For indeed I was stolen away from the land of the Hebrews; and also I have done nothing here that they should put me into the dungeon." —Genesis 40:14-15

Surely, the butler was elated to hear that his life would be spared, and he presumably agreed to mention Joseph to Pharaoh. Three days later, both his dream and the baker's dream came to pass, exactly as Joseph said they would. Both men must have marveled at Joseph's accuracy, and the baker might have wished that it were otherwise. But Joseph's diligence throughout his own ordeal contributed to his personal development. He grew in power and authority and became increasingly bold in his calling and his gift for interpreting dreams, in part because he remained determined to make each moment count.

Knowing that the butler had returned to Pharaoh's presence must have stirred fresh anticipation in Joseph's heart. Surely, he expected the butler to mention him to Pharaoh at the first opportunity. I can almost hear Joseph praying and praising God as he walked back down the prison corridor, saying, "I'm finally going to get out of this place. I'm about to be delivered!"

Of course, that was not the case: "The chief butler did not remember Joseph, but forgot him" (Genesis 40:23). Imagine Joseph's disappointment when nobody showed up to set him free. Yet I believe that during this painful delay, God reminded Joseph that promotion does not come from man but from the Lord. Once again, he had to wait for whatever timing God had established. Instead of curling up in the fetal position and crying his eyes out, Joseph kept doing his job. He remained faithful. He continued in excellence. And he waited on God.

Is that how we respond when we are disappointed? Do we keep doing what we know to do? Or do we pine over the delay and feel sorry for ourselves? May we learn, as Joseph did, to keep pressing on and keep our hearts right with God. We need to allow the Holy Spirit to continue moving in our lives. We need to trust God with the ups, downs, and delays that inevitably come. Then, when it is time for us to lay hold of the blessing, we won't be confused about which end is up. Instead of missing the moments of great opportunity that God has planned for us, let's remember that God's strategic opportunities come after His divine delays, not before.

ENDURING TO THE END

Joseph endured until the end. He knew that he could not make things happen, and certainly not on his timetable. Attempting to dictate his future would have set him up for a long string of disappointments and unnecessary delays. Only God could give him favor in the right places, and only God could open the right doors. Joseph's life might have seemed like a series of calamities, but God placed him in the right places at the right times and arranged opportunities that caused his divine destiny to flourish.

Joseph's unusual and difficult path was perfectly orchestrated by God. Fortunately, Joseph did not allow restlessness to drive him. Nor did he allow difficult circumstances to knock him down. He did not resist God's timing or pry open doors for himself. Doing any of these things could have undone the future that awaited Joseph and the millions whose lives ultimately depended on his destiny being fulfilled.

We can learn so much from Joseph's choice to endure. Every aspect of his conduct that we have studied so far can be applied to some aspect of our lives. His life is more than a matter of history. Joseph's trials, tribulations, and ultimate victory are enlightening. His experiences mirror ours. He was not just a Bible character. He was a man who lived one day at a time, as we do. Whether or not we are called to reach the highest heights as he did, his story is our story. His choice to stand firm can inspire our choices to stand firm. His power to endure can help us find our power to endure.

Joseph's example is vital. Like him, we can be empowered with character, empowered with a heritage, empowered with a dream, empowered to serve, and empowered to endure. When that happens, we are empowered to prosper, as we will see. We can stop striving to lift ourselves to the top. We can rest in God and let Him take us higher than we could ever take ourselves.

I truly believe that enduring is one of the greatest keys to living an anointed lifestyle. It is certainly essential to the fulfillment of our individual callings and our calling as the body of Christ. As we submit to God day by day, He will empower us to endure and to wait. And as we do, we will grow stronger. He will teach us to distinguish and appreciate His divine delays, so we can possess everything that He has prepared for us.

THE SILENT STRENGTH OF ENDURANCE

How is patience completing (or not completing) its perfect work in you? What is your prayer to God for endurance?

Chapter 7

POWER TO PROSPER

As for every man to whom God has given riches and wealth, and given him power to eat of it, to receive his heritage and rejoice in his labor—this is the gift of God.
—Ecclesiastes 5:19

Joseph was a man gifted by God to interpret dreams, to rule, and to prosper. His brothers worshipped the same God that Joseph did, yet they refused to acknowledge the gifts that God had given him. They were concerned about their own power within the family and refused to accept the greatness that God had promised their brother. As far as they were concerned, he was a nuisance, and worse: he was a threat.

In Egypt, pagan men in high places came to recognize the gifts that Joseph's brothers rejected. Because they did, they benefited from Joseph's presence among them. Potiphar saw more than Joseph's ability. He "saw that the LORD *was* with him and that the LORD made all he did to prosper in his hand" (Genesis 39:3). Potiphar wasn't too proud or insecure to affirm Joseph. So, "from the time *that* he had made him overseer of his house and all that he had ... the LORD blessed the Egyptian's house for Joseph's sake; and the blessing of the LORD was on all that he had in the house and in the field" (Genesis 39:5).

Joseph had long known how to interpret dreams. But now he knew how to prosper, and Potiphar wanted in. He knew from the start that Joseph was no ordinary man, but there was no natural way to explain this perception. It was miraculous, really, because Joseph had nothing going for him in the natural sense. Spiritually, however, he had everything he needed to succeed (meaning, to prosper). So, Potiphar gave him an opportunity. He trusted Joseph so completely that he stopped keeping track of his own affairs and "did not know what he had except for the bread which he ate" (Genesis 39:6).

That is more than a matter of trust; it is Potiphar's response to Joseph's ability to prosper. Somehow, Joseph was anointed to manage resources and finances. But how did a young Hebrew slave who arrived in Egypt empty-handed become a man able to create prosperity for the rich and famous? Where did he learn how to manage a large household? How did he learn to invest money and manage personnel? What was at the root of Joseph's power to prosper?

Joseph's success resulted from God's prophetic intention, which would be accomplished in and through Joseph's life. The divine nature caused Joseph and all of Israel to prosper. As long as God's hand was on Joseph, he could prosper anywhere, under any circumstances. God's intention toward him had the power to turn every negative into a positive and every disappointment into a greater opportunity. Joseph's dire circumstances were no match for God's purpose and power, and where Joseph was concerned, God's purpose and power flowed.

PROSPEROUS IN GOD'S EYES

One of the most stunning verses in the Bible is one we have already seen. It is Genesis 39:2, which says, "The LORD was with Joseph, and he was a prosperous man" (KJV). The statement seems out of sync with Joseph's situation. He had just been traded like a head of cattle, first by his brothers and then by Midianite traders. He'd already been sold twice, and if he performed poorly in Potiphar's house, he might be sold again. Instead of being his father's favored son, he was the property of an Egyptian master who ordered him around and even owned him. Joseph was not free to come and go as he pleased. His life of comfort was over. He was a *slave* and seemed to be anything but prosperous.

The usage of the word *prosperous* in Genesis 39:2 conveys the idea of being successful. The verse points to a power to prosper that was not reliant on Joseph's circumstances. He arrived on the selling block with no special name and no resumé. Even his coat was gone. All that Joseph had left were his faith in God, his integrity, and his ability to interpret dreams, which meant nothing to the Egyptians at first. Potiphar would come to appreciate his integrity, and Pharaoh would eventually value his dream interpretation and administrative ability, but none of that changed Joseph's prospects as he was being sold in Egypt.

Nevertheless, the Bible paradoxically states that Joseph was a successful man. This reveals a powerful lesson about prosperity: success or failure as a human being has nothing to do with a person's assets. Joseph's brothers may have stripped him of the coat that represented his favor and coming authority, but they were powerless to remove the actual favor and authority that God had revealed to Joseph. They could not change the fact that even without a dime to his name, Joseph was successful in God's eyes. God knew what the Egyptians would learn over time: He was involved in every detail of Joseph's life. Therefore, Joseph could not help but prosper.

If you are God's, then He is involved in every circumstance of your life. If you look only at your bottom line, you might not see yourself as prosperous. But that doesn't change God's point of view. Stop looking at your situation and start seeing in yourself what God says is there. Don't let the words of your relatives or coworkers cloud your perspective. Do what Joseph did again and again: fix your eyes on God and His prophetic promises. Become determined to cross over the waters of difficulty. Be willing to leave behind any vestige of a maintenance mentality. Make up your mind to enter God's plan regardless of the obstacles. When you do this—when I do this, and God's church does this—the waters will part, and our hands will prosper, just as God intends.

Joseph did not enter his destiny by happenstance. Young as he was, he set his face like flint and did not let himself become overwhelmed by whatever looked hopeless along the way. Don't you be overwhelmed, either! God's prophetic intention for your life never wavers and is not limited by your circumstances. Just agree with His point of view and keep on agreeing! Don't let what looks like misfortune cause your trust in God to falter. If you remain steadfast, it doesn't matter how negative your current situation seems. The outward condition of your life is powerless to nullify God's intentions for you.

Cling to God's prophetic promises. Yes, you will need more resources than you have right now if you are to accomplish all that God has shown you. But He will provide the necessary resources in His own time. Don't let the perception of lack hold you back. Press forward with whatever God has already given you, and the rest will come, right when you need it. He is empowering you to prosper. Now, see in yourself what He sees, and allow Him to prosper you.

THE ANOINTING, FAVOR, AND PROSPERITY

When the sacred anointing oil of the Old Testament was poured upon the head of the priest, it ran down over his garments. The frankincense, cassia, and aloes in the oil were so fragrant that everyone could smell the priest coming, and they knew that he was anointed. God's people will know if you are anointed too. There is no disguising it. When the anointing of God is on you, people take notice.

That is exactly what happened to Joseph in Egypt. The anointing of God did something extraordinary for him, so that "his master saw that the LORD *was* with him and that the LORD made all he did to prosper in his hand" (Genesis 39:3). The next verse says that "Joseph found favor in his sight," and Potiphar then "made him overseer of his house." In other words, the anointing Potiphar saw on Joseph affected how he perceived and received Joseph.

God's anointing attracted Potiphar's favor. God will give you favor in your personal life, and He will give you favor in your business or ministry. He is not shy about His favor; He wants to make it so obvious that no one can deny it. You will not be blessed because you are smarter than other people. You will not be blessed because you try harder than they do. You will be blessed because the Spirit of God is in your life. You are anointed and have the favor of God.

The anointing on Joseph's life brought him favor, and that favor led to his advancement. His rise to the position of overseer at Potiphar's house was meteoric. As a brand-new slave and a foreigner, he could have languished and performed mundane tasks for a lifetime. Instead, he prospered, not monetarily at first but in other ways:

He prospered in favor: because Joseph was granted favor, unusual doors opened for him—doors that led him to serve and gain exposure.

He prospered in opportunities: through the opportunities Joseph was granted, he excelled more and more, developed his skills, and applied them.

He prospered in reputation: Joseph served proactively in every situation and built a good name. As a result, he would one day be mentioned in Pharaoh's court.

Joseph was a patient man who did not despise "the day of small things" (Zechariah 4:10). He discovered that the path to his destiny would be incremental, so he lived with the long game in mind. He also knew his limitations, and he relied on God's anointing to set in motion the things he could not arrange for himself. When Potiphar first recognized Joseph's extraordinary qualities, Joseph was a long way from serving Pharaoh. But he was moving toward his destiny and becoming the man that Pharaoh would need to manage Egypt's food supply when the famine came.

Joseph's prosperity in Egypt was absolutely miraculous, and such miracles are possible for God's people today. Sadly, many Christians never experience them because they are lukewarm toward God and compromise for many reasons. Some make a conscious decision to pull back because they are worried about fitting in and being accepted by others. Some are so preoccupied with the demands of life that they become complacent. Still others put limits on themselves because they don't see themselves through God's eyes. In one way or another, all of them miss out on God's best, as we all do to some extent.

You don't have to forfeit what God generously offers. You just need to know that you are who God says you are and whatever He says is yours *is yours*. Quit worrying about the people who misunderstand you or hate you or throw you into the pit and sell you out. Just walk in the revelation that God's Spirit is with you. Understand that in God's eyes, you are already prosperous, wherever you are and whatever you are doing.

It is time to believe God's plan for your life and rejoice in it. Your life is much bigger than your current moment. If you live an anointed lifestyle, you are empowered to prosper. God's presence in your life will attract favor from every direction, even from perfect strangers. As God's favor opens doors, He will empower you to prosper and excel more and more, guided by the spirit of wisdom that fills your heart and mind with God-given ideas and supernaturally inspired, creative thinking. With every step you take in faith, God will cause you to be the head and not the tail!

PROSPER WHERE YOU ARE

Prosperity is not as much a destination as a determination to see yourself through God's eyes and make each day count, right where you are. True prosperity is a way of living and prospering regardless of your surroundings and shortfalls. I believe Joseph grasped this idea so completely that it empowered him to rise above all his difficulties and succeed in the most unlikely places.

It was not as though Joseph's brothers sent him to Egypt with well wishes and a pocketful of gold coins. When they arranged his departure, they didn't buy him a first-class ticket or reserve him a swanky room in Cairo. They sold him into a life of oppression and danger, and they deprived him of any natural form of provision or defense. Yet, Scripture says that Joseph was a prosperous man. Despite the dangers he faced, despite the privation and his own heartbreak, he prospered in the places that were supposed to destroy him.

That ought to encourage you! I know it does me. It tells me that nothing and nobody can hold us back. Like Joseph, we can make ourselves so useful that we cannot help but be promoted. Like him, we can make the most of every opportunity by excelling and by prospering the people who entrust us with authority. And when people treat us unjustly, we can keep on prospering. Like Joseph, we can end up leading the very people who planned to keep us down.

No person or situation could force Joseph to languish. Wherever he was planted—even against his will—he flourished. Wherever he went, his anointing went with him. Therefore, favor found him in the places where degradation seemed more likely. If that's not a testimony of prosperity, I don't know what is.

Remember that Joseph did not have the privilege of choosing his circumstances. His time in Egypt was forced upon him through betrayal. But he did not allow that to incapacitate him. When Potiphar purchased him as a domestic worker, Joseph knew he was called to bigger things. Yet, he didn't complain about doing household work. He kept looking up and looking ahead. He kept his eyes on the larger picture and on all that God had shown him. He put his hand to whichever plow was given him, and he anticipated what God would do with his obedience. He pressed past his internal objections and shifting emotions because he knew God was faithful.

You and I need to follow Joseph's example by prospering wherever we are. We will always have reasons to be disappointed. Discouragement will come. Maybe your current job is not the "dream job" you were expecting. That doesn't necessarily make it the wrong job for this season. Nor does it mean that you can't prosper while you are there. Don't let your expectations get in the way of your commitment. Excel where you are, and watch what happens.

I am not suggesting that you have to stay in the "wrong job" all your life. I am simply saying that you are empowered by God to prosper, and He often works through circumstances that you would not readily choose. Keep your eyes on Him. He is your source, and He will open doors of prosperity and destiny at just the right time. God will cause you to flourish in ways you have not yet imagined.

SET YOUR MIND STRAIGHT

To prosper, you need to realize that God's plans include you but are bigger than you. Everything God sees and does is beyond what we imagine. I believe He wants to place His people over companies, industries, and new technologies. He wants to put us in places where His intent is not yet being pursued. He wants to show the world His power and excellence, and He wants to bring souls into His kingdom. God has priorities, and we need to make His priorities ours.

Doing that means checking our mindsets. The question "What's in it for me?" is common today, but it's not God's way of thinking. Yet, many people let it guide their choices about whom they should marry, what professions they should choose, and which churches they should attend. The question is emblematic of a mindset that has kept millions—even millions of Christians—from truly prospering.

I cannot find in Scripture where Joseph asked, "What's in it for me?" Based on the choices he made, that question was not in Joseph's mind. Despite his suffering (and maybe even because of his suffering), he was not self-focused or self-serving. If he had been wrapped up in himself, I doubt that he would have gained the trust and respect of people like Potiphar. Having that kind of attitude would have hurt Joseph more than anything else he suffered. Why? Because without the support of influential Egyptians, he would never have had access to people like the butler who had direct access to Pharaoh.

Bear in mind that Joseph wasn't the first person in his bloodline to prosper under difficult circumstances. His grandfather, Abraham, prospered throughout his faith journey and all its difficulties. So did his father, Jacob. Maybe one of the reasons Jacob favored Joseph above his other sons was because he saw in Joseph the mindset that Jacob developed while he was living far from home in his own season of exile.

After Jacob stole his father Isaac's blessing from his brother, Esau (Genesis 27), their mother, Rebekah, learned that Esau planned to kill Jacob. She immediately advised Jacob to flee to Haran, where her brother Laban lived (Genesis 27:43). Jacob lived in virtual exile for twenty years and served his uncle Laban, who became his father-in-law.

Jacob kept Laban's flocks and did it faithfully. But Laban was a deceiver in his own right. He repeatedly cheated Jacob: he tricked him into marrying his daughter Leah; he often changed Jacob's wages; and he blocked Jacob's attempts to start out on his own with his growing family. Laban did all this even though Jacob's faithfulness had made Laban wealthier than he had been before Jacob showed up. (How similar this scenario is to Joseph's story with Potiphar!)

While Jacob was in Haran, Laban's household was blessed, and Laban recognized God's anointing on Jacob. And even though Laban undermined him, he could not prevent Jacob from prospering.

Not only did Jacob prosper materially in Haran, but he also matured throughout his exile. His transformation began when he encountered God through a dream he had on his way to Haran (Genesis 28:10-22). It continued as he pressed past Laban's injustices and led his family throughout their time in Haran (Genesis 29-31). Jacob would be transformed yet again after he left Laban and wrestled with God at Peniel (Genesis 32:24-30).

Jacob left a trail of blessings behind him. Decades later, Joseph continued in his father's tradition of bringing God's blessing to those around him. It didn't matter that Potiphar was a pagan who worshipped false gods. Potiphar could not help but be blessed as long as Joseph was around. The anointing that was on Joseph empowered his own prosperity and equipped him to prosper others, just as his father had done.

Joseph's mindset cooperated with God's empowerment to prosper. But the "what's in it for me" attitude is the kind of mindset that opposes godly prosperity. So is the persecution complex that affects many Christians who seem to grow up expecting to be rejected. They are consciously or unconsciously convinced that they cannot succeed in this life. Therefore, they don't.

Joseph *was* persecuted, but he remained convinced that success was his portion. When his brothers rejected his gift, he found people—perfect strangers—who would recognize it. When one door slammed shut, he looked for the next door to open. When the unfolding of his dreams led to a series of seeming nightmares, he kept believing God to preserve His prophetic promise and fulfill it.

You may be in a season of unusual tests and trials, but if you keep your thinking straight, your troubles cannot destroy you. Let your tests and trials refine you like gold (Zechariah 13:9). Let your darkest days be seasons of inner growth and maturation. Remember that God's anointing will cause His favor to follow you. He will make you prosper despite everything that comes against you.

NEVER RELINQUISH YOUR POWER TO PROSPER

Life is no bed of roses. Just ask Joseph. At home in his father's house, it looked like Joseph had it made. Then, his world came crashing down around him. He found himself in a pitched battle with the spirit of antichrist, fighting for his identity and destiny in God. Joseph believed what God had shown him about who he was and who he would become. But in their rage and insecurity, his brothers sought to keep Joseph from everything past, present, and future. They were even prepared to shed his blood.

Despite their best efforts, Joseph's brothers could not prevent him from prospering. He was more resilient than they could have imagined. Despite the betrayals and satanically inspired attacks, Joseph held onto his gift. He also held onto his anointing, his prophetic promise, and his identity. He refused to relinquish his power to prosper, and he contended for his God-ordained destiny. Because Joseph would not quit, he won.

You too are anointed and destined to arise. Jesus, the Alpha and the Omega, the Beginning and the End, the First and the Last, the Lily of the Valley, the Bright and Morning Star, and the Blessed Rose of Sharon has a plan for you to prosper. No one can destroy that plan unless you relinquish it.

Never mind the unkind things someone said about you. Never mind those who say you don't have what it takes to fulfill the vision God gave you. You may have heard all your life that you would never amount to anything. Maybe they said you were not as intelligent as your siblings or your classmates. You heard that lie so often that you began to believe it, and it has become a mindset that prevents you from prospering.

Stop listening to what everyone else says and start meditating on what God says about you. You were not destined to live in slavery. You were destined to rule. You are empowered with a prophetic dream. You are anointed and favored of God. If you will see Him for who He is and believe who He says you are, nobody will prevent you from achieving all that God has called you to achieve. The Savior is with you and in you. The Healer is with you and in you. The Baptizer in the Holy Ghost is with you and in you. Jehovah Jireh, your Provider, is with you and in you. Jehovah Shalom, the Lord of Peace, is with you and in you. El Shaddai, God Almighty, has taken up residence in your life, and there is no way you can fail.

If you are His, you are destined for success. You are empowered to prosper, and no one—absolutely *no one*—can stop you.

ANOINTED TO PROSPER

What do you think you lack in the natural sense? What do you possess in the spiritual sense that makes all the difference, and how has that difference already manifested in your life?

Part 3

READY

to

REIGN

Chapter 8

EMPOWERED FOR THE CALL

The gifts and the calling of God are irrevocable.
—Romans 11:29

W hen God calls, He empowers. Where God calls, He provides. He will not call you and withhold the ability to obey Him. He will enable you to prosper in whatever He asks you to do. If you say you are called to a specific area of kingdom work but seem to lack God's power to succeed in that work, something is wrong. Either you are not called, or you don't yet have a revelation of what the Holy Spirit has done in you. If you are not called in that specific area, then you are called to something else. But if you are lacking in revelation, the power is already there, waiting for you to discover and use it.

He who has called you is faithful (1 Thessalonians 5:24). He will not call you to serve and then tie your hands. He will not keep from you the power to prosper in your assignment. He is good, just, and generous. You can trust Him.

EMPOWERED: PROCLAMATION AND DEMONSTRATION

We Christians sometimes believe that certain callings require less of the Holy Spirit's power than other callings do. The truth is that we need the Spirit's power in all things. Even witnessing to your best friend requires divine empowerment. We always need the Holy Spirit to do the work in and through us.

Acts 1:8 says, "You shall receive power when the Holy Spirit has come upon you; and you shall be witnesses to Me in Jerusalem, and in all Judea and Samaria, and to the end of the earth." Here, Jesus promised the empowerment that made witnesses out of the earliest believers and still makes witnesses out of us. But witnessing is more than testifying and sharing Scripture verses. The proclamation requires a demonstration. We need the gift of the Holy Spirit so the evidence of Christ's life and anointing can be manifested. Having the right words to say is important, but the manifestations that come by the Spirit are the proof of what you are saying.

Paul told the Corinthians: "You are our epistle written in our hearts, known and read by all men; clearly you are an epistle of Christ, ministered by us, written not with ink but by the Spirit of the living God, not on tablets of stone but on tablets of flesh, *that is*, of the heart" (2 Corinthians 3:2-3). We are now epistles—*you* are an epistle, written not with ink but by the Spirit, who has written on the tablet of your heart! Scripture doesn't say that you are a living epistle *heard by all men.* It says you are to be "known and read by all men." If you are God's witness, a demonstration of His power in and through your life will speak for itself. People will know that there is "something about you," the way that Potiphar and his wife knew there was something about Joseph. People will see how the anointing makes you different. They will notice how it changes the way you walk, talk, think, and act.

You will notice it too. You will not be afraid of demons, disease, or depression. You will have supernatural boldness and look beyond the rebukes and rejection of others. You will become a living demonstration of the gospel you share. Even if those to whom you witness don't understand what they are sensing or what the anointing is, they will discern that you have what it takes to lift burdens and destroy yokes.

Whatever your calling—whether to ministry, parenthood, leadership, business, or all of the above—you have more than the call in you. You also have the power to fulfill that call and to accomplish the purpose of God for your life. The call and the power are like twins in the womb: they are always together. When God gives one, He gives the other, without fail. If He calls you, He gifts you. If He gifts you, He empowers you to use the gift. Whether your call is to teach a class, go to the mission field, or lay hands on the sick, you can count on an impartation of Holy Ghost power to come specifically for that task. Your proclamation will be matched by the Spirit's demonstration. That is God's promise.

EMPOWERED FOR HIS PURPOSE

God will empower you but always with purpose. He sees your call and gifts in relation to what He intends to do in the earth. He knows what He intends to accomplish through you. He will send you out but never alone. He goes with you. After all, His Spirit is *in you*. When He says, "This is the work I have set before you," He doesn't just pack your lunch and cut you loose. He becomes responsible for the outcome and makes sure you are equipped to succeed.

There is this word of caution, however: only God can call you, and only He can anoint you. You have a spiritual destination in Him, and only He can take you there. If you try to call yourself or assign yourself to a certain spiritual destination without an anointing from God, your efforts will be futile, and your failure will not be God's fault. Unless you are truly called, you will not be empowered. You will be divinely gifted for *something* in this life but not for anything you have appointed yourself to do. Without God's calling and power, you will only end up frustrated, and the work you are trying to do will prove impossible. If you insist on doing it anyway, it will ultimately break you.

If you are diligently toiling—in the ministry, on the mission field, or in a certain industry—and are not seeing any manifestation of God's giftings and empowerment, ask yourself where the call came from. Maybe you went to Bible school, which is wonderful. But studying at Bible school is not evidence that you are called to be a preacher any more than sitting in a garage proves you were called to be a car. Likewise, keeping company with a group of people who operate in the prophetic realm is not the test of whether you are called to be a prophet. The calling of God is not something you catch from other people; it is something you are given by God.

It is true that you can receive spiritual impartation and tutelage from anointed men and women of God. But only God can anoint you, and He will do it before He sends you. He is the One who distributes His gifts, and only He can equip those He calls with the power needed to fulfill His intended purpose.

You will be divinely gifted for something in this life but not for anything you have appointed yourself to do. Without God's calling and power, you will only end up frustrated, and the work you are trying to do will prove impossible.

THE ANOINTING: *ENCHRIO* AND *EPICHRIO*

The anointing is critical to the call and warrants a close look. In the simplest terms, the anointing is an empowerment from God that allows a natural man or woman to act supernaturally. The English word *anointing* is translated from the Greek work *chrio*, which means "to smear or rub with oil."[6] In Old Testament times, oil was used to anoint those who would serve God in any capacity. The power was not in the oil; however, the oil was symbolic of the Holy Spirit who empowers God's people to act.

When speaking of the anointing, the Bible uses some derivatives of the root word *chrio*. One is e*nchrio*, which means "to rub in" (as to rub in the oil).[7] The *enchrio* anointing is for

---

6   Bible Tools, accessed October 6, 2023, s.v. "chrio" (Strongs #5548), https://www.bibletools.org/index.cfm/fuseaction/Lexicon.show/ID/G5548/chrio.htm#:~:text=chri%C5%8D,Part%20of%20Speech%3A%20verb.

7   StudyLight, accessed October 6, 2023, s.v. "enchrio" (Strong's #1472), https://www.studylight.org/dictionaries/eng/ved/a/anoint-anointing.html.

our personal edification as God works in us. Another word is *epichrio* from the same root, which denotes "to rub on."[8] This refers to the anointing that is upon us to minister to others. The rubbing in and rubbing on are equally important and work together to accomplish the fullness of God's intent.

THE *ENCHRIO*

The *enchrio* is the anointing placed in you *for you*. The express purpose of this Holy Spirit deposit is to enrich your personal life and walk with Christ. Jesus said, "I counsel you to buy from Me gold refined in the fire, that you may be rich; and white garments, that you may be clothed, that the shame of your nakedness may not be revealed; and anoint your eyes with eye salve, that you may see" (Revelation 3:18). The *eyes* and *eye salve* here do not refer to the natural eyes; they speak of the spiritual eyes. When God's *enchrio* anointing is applied to your life, it enhances your spiritual sight and sharpens your spiritual hearing. This in turn enriches your relationship with Him and supports your spiritual development.

John wrote, "He who has an ear, let him hear what the Spirit says to the churches. To him who overcomes I will give to eat from the tree of life, which is in the midst of the Paradise of God" (Revelation 2:7). Have you noticed that it is possible to have ears but not hear? The *enchrio* spiritually empowers the inner person and better aligns us with the things of God. This inner work not only enables us to follow Christ; it empowers us to become like Him—anointed like Him, sharing in what He has, and living in ways that reflect His life in us.

---

8   Ibid., s.v. "epichrio" (Strong's #2025).

Enchrio (the rubbing *in*) will empower and conform you to the image of Christ. Consider how its transformative effects are already working in your life:

Enchrio affects your thinking. Paul wrote, "Let this mind be in you which was also in Christ Jesus" (Philippians 2:5). The mind of Jesus Christ, the Anointed One, is inherently anointed. God is calling each of us to seek the anointing that can dramatically change our thinking and, therefore, our outcomes in life.

The *enchrio* brings holiness. If you receive the rubbing in of the anointing that impacts your inner man by the authority, power, favor, holiness, and virtue of the Lord God, you will no longer find it difficult to live right. Where the *enchrio* is concerned, you only receive what you are open to receiving. Joseph had an open heart toward God that allowed the revelation of God to be conceived inside him. God responded to Joseph's openness by continuing to work through him.

The *enchrio* brings blessing. Think about the story of the twelve spies in Numbers 13. Ten spies rejected God's promise, but Joshua and Caleb held fast and insisted on taking the Promised Land. In Joshua, the Lord saw a man in whom the Spirit was evident, a man He could entrust with greater empowerment. So, He declared a blessing upon Joshua (Joshua 1:3-5). The Lord also saw that Caleb had a different spirit from the ten complaining spies because the Holy Spirit was inside him. Therefore, God said that Caleb and his seed would possess the land (Numbers 14:24). Because of the *enchrio*, these men were blessed and more than able to fulfill their destinies in God.

The *enchrio* brings revelation. It also empowers you to prepare for and arrive at your destination in God. When a revelation comes to you through a pastor or prophet, it might reach your spirit, but it must first be processed through your intellect so that you can judge whether it is from God. But when the Holy Ghost speaks to you directly, the words will burn in your spirit, and the message conveyed by those words will shake you from the crown of your head to the soles of your feet. Your *enchrio* brings revelation, which changes you from the inside out.

The *enchrio* brings edification. Have you ever felt so beat up that you were at a loss to talk to God? That is when the Holy Spirit takes over. Suddenly, your anointing starts stirring and your hands start reaching toward heaven. Your flesh says, *I don't want to pray*, but your anointing begins to bubble and stir deep inside you. Suddenly, you are built up, strengthened, encouraged, and ready to devote yourself to the integrity of God. In difficult times, the *enchrio* will fortify every muscle in your spiritual anatomy.

The *enchrio* protects you from falling. It is the inner anointing that keeps your character in shape and keeps you spiritually whole. If you faithfully attend to the deposit that God has placed within you—acknowledging it, protecting it, and allowing it to flow through you—you will not become spiritually stagnant or fall by the wayside. You won't hit a certain level and wonder why you can't go any higher. As you steward your *enchrio*, you will stand and keep on standing in faith.

While the *enchrio* and *epichrio* are equally important, you must have the first to properly flow in the second. God first wants to form you and establish godly character in your spirit. This is how He empowers you to walk in the image and likeness of Christ. The man or woman with the greater *enchrio* will have the greater *epichrio*. Those who have the greater anointing *in* them will walk with a greater anointing *upon* them to work the works of God.

THE *EPICHRIO*

Remember that the *epichrio* (the rubbing on of the anointing) is the deposit of God's power upon your life that enables you to minister to others. This empowerment works with the character-developing *enchrio* anointing to demonstrate that God is working in and through the call on your life.

Look at this verse from John's Gospel: "When [Jesus] had said these things, He spat on the ground and made clay with the saliva; and He anointed the eyes of the blind man with the clay" (John 9:6). The word translated "anointed" in this verse is *epichrio*. When Jesus physically rubbed the clay and saliva mixture on the man's eyes, a supernatural change occurred, and the man regained his sight. He was not changed inwardly; he was changed outwardly.

There is nothing quite like the *epichrio* experience. When it operates, you will feel like the prophet Elijah did when he outran the chariots (1 Kings 18:46). You will sense the strength to carry the gates of the city on your shoulders, the way Samson did in Gaza (Judges 16:3). The powerful *epichrio* anointing will permanently change your life.

The *epichrio* transforms your emotions, including fear. When the Lord first approached Gideon in the winepress, the man was weak, afraid of his enemies, and unsure of himself. After God revealed His purpose to Gideon, and the Spirit came upon him, Gideon's former frailties vanished, and he was supernaturally empowered to fulfill his call. (See Judges 6:11-8:28.)

The *epichrio* causes you to give whatever you have to fulfill God's purposes. When Peter and John were en route to the temple to pray, they came upon a lame man at the entrance of the holy place. According to the Scriptures, the man had been "lame from his mother's womb" (Acts 3:2). However, Peter and John had an *epichrio* on them and were dripping with Holy Ghost oil. They were ready and supernaturally empowered to help somebody get free of any burdens and yokes. They had something to give the lame man: it was the *epichrio* that enabled them to fulfill God's intention for him.

The *epichrio* is for the here and now. You won't need the anointing to help others when you get to heaven. There will be no one left to heal because there won't be any sickness there. Moving in the prophetic gift will not be necessary either because in heaven God's people will "know just as [they] also [are] known" (1 Corinthians 13:12). The *epichrio* is for right now and serves the purposes you were anointed to fulfill in the earth. When the Holy Spirit is poured on you, you can hear God's voice speaking to your heart and then discern what He is saying about ministry to others. To operate in His supernatural power is to operate in faith, which is necessary to seize the opportunities He presents. Then, you will accomplish whatever He is asking of you.

The *epichrio* allows you to witness with power, preach with conviction, lay hands on the sick or bound, and see supernatural results. When the Spirit of God comes upon you to serve others, you can feel His supernatural presence. Suddenly, the negative circumstances you face won't matter. You are free to fulfill His purposes and minister in His power, regardless of the opposition that is organized against you.

Just as the *enchrio* in you must be properly attended to so that you can remain spiritually strong, the *epichrio* must be acted upon so that you can accomplish supernatural feats for God. It is not a gift to be saved for a special occasion or a more convenient time. Your *epichrio* is active and will enable you to do the "greater works" that Jesus promised (John 14:12).

THE PURPOSE OF THE ANOINTING

In biblical days, the act of anointing someone with oil was the means of transferring divine power and authority to that person. It also represented a bestowal of God's favor and an impartation of His holiness and virtue. These dynamics of the anointing of God—power, authority, favor, holiness, and virtue—comprise the empowerment that God gives to His children so they can live victorious lives and carry out His work in the earth.

The anointing's purpose is pictured in this verse from the Book of Isaiah: "It shall come to pass in that day *That* [the Assyrian's] burden will be taken away from your shoulder, and his yoke from your neck, and the yoke will be destroyed because of the anointing oil" (Isaiah 10:27). When the anointing is present, burdens are removed and yokes are destroyed. You can recognize when the anointing is present because you can bear witness to what it accomplishes.

You can apply this idea to what you already know about the *enchrio* and the *epichrio*. The purpose of the *enchrio* is to lift personal burdens and destroy yokes in your personal life. The purpose of the *epichrio* is to lift the burdens and destroy the yokes of the people to whom you minister. When you are anointed, you bring God's power, authority, favor, holiness, and virtue to bear. In whatever situation you are called to address, you do the works of Christ, the Anointed One. Anything that is done in His power, authority, favor, holiness, and virtue results in the lifting of burdens and the destruction of yokes. That is the law of the anointing.

The Hebrew word used for anointing in Isaiah 10:27 is unique. It is only used in this verse and in Psalms 23. It is *semen,* which translates as "richness" or "fatness."[9] When you are genuinely empowered by God, you are enriched and enlarged. Your destiny in Him is far greater than your destiny apart from Him. He helps you in indescribable ways and increases you beyond anything you might expect. He knows that you can't fulfill His call upon your life when you are burdened or shackled. So, His anointing frees you to free others. Instead of being preoccupied with your troubles, He expands your vision and extends it outward to serve and set others free.

9   Blue Letter Bible, s.v. "semen," accessed September 26, 2023, https://www.blueletterbible.org/lexicon/h8081/kjv/wlc/0-1/.

In the context of Isaiah 10:27, Israel was an anointed nation. Yet, at times, she found herself under the yoke of foreign enemies. In this case, the Assyrians were oppressing God's people. However, God said that the burden would be lifted, and the yoke would be destroyed because of the anointing—the power, authority, favor, virtue, and holiness of God. His people would be free because of the greatness and richness of the One who had anointed them.

As we move in our individual callings, we need to understand why God has anointed us and what He wants to accomplish. This requires us to look beyond the sensations we experience under His anointing. He empowers us this way because He has in mind an eternal destiny that is larger than what we see in the current moment. Our lives are to be marked by signs, wonders, and miracles that attest to Him. We are destined to see His hand at work. We see His kingdom coming in burden-lifting, yoke-destroying visitations that touch our own lives and the lives of the people around us.

God has amazing plans for you. He wants to lift your burden and break your yoke because of the calling that is upon your life and because of the sacred destiny He has pronounced over you. He is committed to His purposes, and you are included in His plans.

ONLY ONE SOURCE

Remember that the oil is not the source of God's power but a symbol of it. You cannot anoint yourself with oil and expect His power to flow. Nothing in your mind, flesh, or emotions can empower you to do the work of God. The anointing cannot be drummed up or conceived through your emotions or intellect. Although you might feel the anointing when it is upon you, the anointing itself does not rely on your feelings. God's enabling power exists whether you feel it or not.

The anointing is not found in knowledge, education, the right school, or even the right seminary. The anointing is not determined by your position in the community. It has nothing to do with your financial success, employment status, or possessions. Your appearance, church attendance, virtues, personality, and talents do not qualify you for the anointing. God can anoint your personality and natural talents and make them effective for Him, but your personality and talents don't make you anointed. No matter how anointed your mother is, and no matter how long she stays on her knees interceding for you, it is still God who must do the anointing. Without Him, you are nothing, and I am nothing.

Our trust cannot be in ourselves but only in God. We depend on His anointing, knowing that without it, we are powerless to serve Him. Even Jesus depended on the Father for His anointing. In Luke 4, Jesus stood up in the synagogue to give the day's reading, which was from the Book of Isaiah. The passage spoke of the Messiah and the purpose of the anointing He received:

> *The Spirit of the LORD GOD is upon Me,*
> *Because the LORD has anointed Me*
> *To preach good tidings to the poor;*
> *He has sent Me to heal the brokenhearted,*
> *To proclaim liberty to the captives,*

And the opening of the prison to those who are bound;
To proclaim the acceptable year of the LORD,
And the day of vengeance of our God.
—Isaiah 61:1-2

There is no record of Jesus having worked any miracles before He was thirty years of age. The first recorded miracle in His ministry took place after He arose from the waters of His baptism in the Jordan River, "and the Holy Spirit descended in bodily form like a dove upon Him" (Luke 3:22). From that moment on, Jesus could honestly say, "The Spirit of the LORD GOD *is* upon Me" (Isaiah 61:1). Shortly after His baptism, miraculous things began to happen in Jesus's life and ministry. He understood and respected the role of the anointing in the fulfillment of His mission.

THREE LEVELS OF ANOINTING

To arrive at the place of power and authority that God has destined for us, we must pass through three levels or phases of the anointing: the anointing of revelation, the anointing of preparation, and the anointing of destination.

The Anointing of Revelation

Possibly the most fundamental and essential revelation is the one declared in Romans 8:16-17: "The Spirit Himself bears witness with our spirit that we are children of God, and if children, then heirs—heirs of God and joint heirs with Christ, if indeed we suffer with *Him*, that we may also be glorified together."

Until we have received the revelation of who we are in God and of His eternal plan for our lives, we are not fully alive. Receiving this revelation is like the conceiving of a seed that yields life in the womb. Paul wrote that the Spirit "bears witness with our spirit that we are children of God." This describes a coming together of the human spirit with God's Spirit. Without that union, there can be no spiritual life and no God-ordained purpose for our existence. As God speaks to us about the things He wants us to do with our lives, we cry out from the depths of the human spirit to conceive the revelation and life that only the Holy Spirit can bring.

Consider this reality in light of your call and the following passage from Romans:

> *The earnest expectation of the creation eagerly waits for the revealing of the sons of God. For the creation was subjected to futility, not willingly, but because of Him who subjected it in hope; because the creation itself also will be delivered from the bondage of corruption into the glorious liberty of the children of God. For we know that the whole creation groans and labors with birth pangs together until now. Not only that, but we also who have the firstfruits of the Spirit, even we ourselves groan within ourselves, eagerly waiting for the adoption, the redemption of our body. —Romans 8:19-23*

The way Paul explains it, your spirit cries out, *I am here! My purpose is to be united with the Spirit of God. Only then can I be fruitful.* When you come into agreement with God and your spirit unites with His Spirit, new life comes forth. When

He speaks into your life through a vision, dream, prophetic word, or divine revelation, you sense His empowering presence touching your life.

As soon as you conceive the anointing of revelation, you receive a transferring, or impartation. His power is made available to you, so that you can prepare to step into your destiny in Him. Notice that the revelation precedes the impartation. Immediately after the revelation, the anointing puts your faith into operation and begins working within you to lift any burdens, destroy any yokes, and abolish all spirits of fear, hopelessness, and confusion.

Of course, the devil wants to abort your anointing of revelation and seeks every opportunity to do so. He knows that while your spirit is crying out to conceive, your carnal mind is open to ways of preventing the revelation from coming to full term. Why? Because the flesh prefers not to pay the price of conception; it would rather continue in your present comfort zone, even though the slavery of comfort will kill the dream, vision, and plan of God for your life.

Satan plays on this inner conflict. As you ponder what God reveals, Satan strategizes. He knows God's word to you is true, so he launches his attack swiftly, deploying one of his weapons of choice: the feeling of hopelessness. He tries to bog you down with regrets about your past defeats and current chaos. He knows full well that the anointing of revelation is not contingent upon your situation or track record. But he also knows that immersing you deep in hopelessness might convince you that you are disqualified from moving forward.

Don't be deceived. Anything the devil says or tries to prove is a lie. Reject it! Allow the seed of the revelation God gave you to be conceived in your spiritual womb. There is nothing more that you need to do. Just let that seed flourish and allow God to do the rest.

As soon as you conceive the anointing of revelation, you receive a transferring, or impartation. His power is made available to you, so that you can prepare to step into your destiny in Him.

The Anointing of Preparation

After Samuel poured the anointing oil over David (1 Samuel 16:13), David entered a very difficult period of preparation. Instead of fending for himself and doing things his way, he had to release his desire for control and be led by God's Spirit. David endured some very difficult situations, but he learned to radically trust God, which was critical to his destiny. God was preparing him for greatness, and his period of preparation was nonnegotiable.

What David experienced in this difficult season is typical of what we experience in ours. Once we receive the anointing of revelation, know that we are the children of God, and understand our destiny in Him, God takes off the kid gloves and deals with us firmly. We might shrink from this chastening, but it is a necessary part of our training as His legitimate children. The writer of Hebrews explains:

My son, do not despise the chastening of the LORD,
Nor be discouraged when you are rebuked by Him;
For whom the LORD loves He chastens,

And scourges every son whom He receives.
If you endure chastening, God deals with you as with
sons . . . But if you are without chastening . . . then
you are illegitimate and not sons. —Hebrews 12:5-8

If we expect to rise to the fullness of our destinies in God, we have to allow time for the anointing to deal with the weaknesses of our flesh, emotions, and attitudes. To bypass this step is to compromise our spiritual well-being and future resilience. Unless we cooperate as the Spirit of God builds the *enchrio* within us, we can end up like King Saul—misguided, disoriented, rejected of God, and divested of all divine authority. If we choose to remain immature, we cannot possess our prophetic heritage, and our destinies will fall by the wayside.

Joseph learned this lesson very well. He endured his protracted anointing of preparation. He had to pass through the pit and the prison before his revelation and destiny became reality. At times, he might have felt forgotten by God, as we also do. But God had not forgotten him and has not forgotten us. God is dealing firmly with us and making us ready for greater things.

The Anointing of Destination

Regardless of your age or what you have already accomplished for God, you still have a destination in Him. Joseph's anointing of destination was essential to his godly lifestyle. His brothers meant to destroy him, but God had anointed him with his destination in mind. Joseph moved toward that destination, both in his father's house and during his years in Egypt.

It is not as though Joseph had "arrived" on the day Pharaoh appointed him as his second in command. In fact, what God had prepared Joseph to undertake was just beginning. The famine had not yet begun, and Joseph had to prepare Egypt ahead of time. Then, when the famine began, Joseph's responsibilities expanded. The full benefits of his call—for him, for Egypt, and for his own family—were only starting to unfold.

The full benefits of your call are still ahead. God will anoint you for a specific day and hour that He has prepared for you—if you are willing to pay whatever price comes with His call. So, what is the price of walking in an anointing of destination? Simply put, the price is responsibility. As you know, your everyday responsibilities often violate aspects of your personal life and preferences. Responsibilities are inconvenient and generally unwilling to wait. Similarly, when rivers of living water dwell in your innermost being, you have a responsibility to pour them out, not at a time of your choosing but at the appointed time. To deal with that, you have to unseat your flesh from its natural position as lord of your life and enthrone the Lord Jesus there instead.

When you step into your anointing of destination, you will know it. Something supernatural will happen at a level that is new to you. A very different kind of power will come through your ministry, and it will flourish. Your anointing and the obedience that brought the anointing to your life will become more important to you than anything else. Your priorities will change, and your level of commitment to the things of God will rise.

Being anointed for the call is serious business. Cooperating with God at this level demands a singleness of focus and submission that causes many people to draw back. Being anointed for the call requires something more than you might expect, at times when you feel least prepared to give it. You might pass through some long days and sleepless nights. But in the final analysis, the price will be nothing when compared with the glorious completion of your call. There is no better, higher, or more rewarding life than this!

EMPOWERED FROM THE INSIDE OUT

A proclamation requires a demonstration. From the perspective of the anointing, how have your *enchrio* and *epichrio* worked together to demonstrate the gospel?

Chapter 9

THE *KAIROS* MOMENT

Let us not grow weary while doing good, for in due season we shall reap if we do not lose heart.
—Galatians 6:9

Two years after Joseph interpreted the dreams of the butler and the baker, the butler's troubles seemed to be over, and he was back to serving in Pharaoh's court. Joseph, however, was exactly where the butler left him—in Pharaoh's prison, with no indication of a breakthrough. Joseph had asked that the butler mention him to Pharaoh, "yet the chief butler did not remember Joseph, but forgot him" (Genesis 40:23).

God had not forgotten Joseph. He was with him, preparing him and his gift for a particular moment—a *kairos* moment in which Joseph would be called into royal service in an astounding and life-transforming way. *Kairos* is more than a moment in chronological time; it is a moment in God's ordained timing—an "opportune"[10] or "propitious

---

10 Blue Letter Bible, s.v. "kairos," accessed April 22, 2024, https://www.blueletterbible.org/lexicon/g2540/kjv/tr/0-1/.

moment"[11] in which opportunity and possibility converge in the unfolding of divine purpose. Joseph's *kairos* moment came when the world's most powerful leader became troubled by two significant dreams—one about seven fat cows and seven lean ones, and a second dream about seven plump heads of grain and seven scrawny ones (Genesis 41:2-7). Powerful as he was, Pharaoh could not shake loose of the dreams or his sense of foreboding. And none of his advisors or magicians could even tell him what the dreams meant.

Suddenly, the chief butler remembered the Hebrew man who had interpreted his own troubling dream, and he did the one thing that Joseph had asked of him:

> *[He] spoke to Pharaoh, saying: "I remember my faults this day. When Pharaoh was angry with his servants, and put me in custody in the house of the captain of the guard, both me and the chief baker, we each had a dream in one night, he and I. Each of us dreamed according to the interpretation of his own dream. Now there was a young Hebrew man with us there, a servant of the captain of the guard. And we told him, and he interpreted our dreams for us; to each man he interpreted according to his own dream. And it came to pass, just as he interpreted for us, so it happened. He restored me to my office, and he hanged him." —Genesis 41:9-13*

In the perfection of divine timing, the butler repented of his oversight and made the introduction for which Joseph had

---

11 Google's English Dictionary, s.v. "kairos," accessed April 22, 2024, https://www.google.com/search?q=definition+of+kairos.

been hoping. In retrospect, the excruciating two-year delay was not a curse but a blessing.

WHEN YOUR MOMENT COMES

In God, there was an appointed time for Joseph's ascent, and it was now. God had long since gifted Joseph to interpret dreams. Now, He arranged for Joseph to put his gift to work in a spectacular way. Yet again, Joseph became a blessing to others—not only to Pharaoh in this case but to all of Egypt, to Israel, and to every person whose life would be saved by Joseph's wisdom.

The prophetic promise wrapped in Joseph's dreams did not unfold in rapid or predictable timing. But it manifested in divine order. "Then Pharaoh sent and called Joseph, and they brought him quickly out of the dungeon; and he shaved, changed his clothing, and came to Pharaoh" (Genesis 41:14).

Imagine the force of that moment for Joseph and the flood of feelings and emotions that coursed through his being. As monumental as the moment was, the only thing left for him to do was to shave, change his clothing, and show up. He had been preparing for just such a moment all his life. Now, God had opened a great door and given Joseph access to Pharaoh himself.

Joseph was about to step through that door and into his promised destiny. What seemed so distant from the dungeon was now only footsteps away. Finally, Joseph stood before Pharaoh, the man whose bonds had held him captive. Joseph was not there to plead his case or beg for mercy. He was summoned to serve God's purposes. So, he listened as the mighty

Pharaoh explained his predicament: "I have had a dream," said Pharaoh, "and *there is* no one who can interpret it. But I have heard it said of you *that* you can understand a dream, to interpret it" (Genesis 41:15).

Pharaoh laid bare his distress before a man he did not know—a seemingly powerless Hebrew, an alien, slave, and inmate. Another man in Joseph's shoes might have exploited Pharaoh's transparency. He might have touted himself before the court and leveraged Pharaoh's fears. But not Joseph. He was not there to cash in or gain the upper hand. He simply humbled himself and set the record straight. He told Pharaoh that any wisdom or strength he could offer came only from God, the One whose power exceeded all other power. Of the interpretation Pharaoh needed, Joseph calmly said, "*It is* not in me; God will give Pharaoh an answer of peace'" (Genesis 41:16).

Joseph now stood on the threshold of his prophetic promise. When he awakened that morning, he did not know that his gifts would be called upon before day's end. Through years of waiting, he could not know when his day of promise would come. He had asked the butler to speak to Pharaoh on his behalf, but he had no guarantee that Pharaoh would be his liberator. Until he was summoned, Joseph was not privy to Pharaoh's dreams or his failed attempts to have them interpreted. Only God knew of the wonders He was working.

Although Joseph had anticipated his breakthrough, experiencing it was surely electrifying.

Yet Joseph had to remain clear-headed. He knew that the God who was with him in the pit, in Potiphar's house, and in the prison was with him now. So, as Pharaoh recounted his dreams, Joseph stood silent and relied on God's Spirit for the interpretation. The fact that someone as powerful as Pharaoh was expecting an answer did not seem to fluster Joseph, although he surely understood the implications of the moment.

Amazingly, Joseph did not hesitate to answer Pharaoh. He needed no additional time to consider his reply or pray for clarity. He was anointed, and his gift was in operation, just as it had been at other times and in other places. So, with all composure, he interpreted Pharaoh's dreams:

> *"This is the thing which I have spoken to Pharaoh. God has shown Pharaoh what He is about to do. Indeed seven years of great plenty will come throughout all the land of Egypt; but after them seven years of famine will arise, and all the plenty will be forgotten in the land of Egypt; and the famine will deplete the land. So the plenty will not be known in the land because of the famine following, for it will be very severe. And the dream was repeated to Pharaoh twice because the thing is established by God, and God will shortly bring it to pass." —Genesis 41:28-32*

What a staggering reminder this passage is of how all things are possible with God! (See Matthew 19:26.) Joseph knew that Pharaoh's dreams were not random; they had come for a reason. And because Joseph had been summoned, it was clear that God intended to reveal the reason through Joseph. Only God could meet Pharaoh's need, but Joseph would deliver God's message.

Without the slightest stammer, Joseph boldly told Pharaoh exactly what he needed to do:

"Now therefore, let Pharaoh select a discerning and wise man, and set him over the land of Egypt. Let Pharaoh do this, and let him appoint officers over the land, to collect one-fifth of the produce of the land of Egypt in the seven plentiful years. And let them gather all the food of those good years that are coming, and store up grain under the authority of Pharaoh, and let them keep food in the cities. Then that food shall be as a reserve for the land for the seven years of famine which shall be in the land of Egypt, that the land may not perish during the famine." —Genesis 41:33-36

As Joseph delivered God's answer, the anointing delivered Pharaoh from the yoke of oppression his dreams had laid upon him. No wonder he was impressed by Joseph! He recognized God's anointing and acknowledged it in no uncertain terms. He was not only liberated but exuberant. He asked everyone present, "Can we find *such a one* as this, a man in whom *is* the Spirit of God?" (Genesis 41:38)

Then, Pharaoh said to Joseph:

"Inasmuch as God has shown you all this, there is no one as discerning and wise as you. You shall be over my house, and all my people shall be ruled according to your word; only in regard to the throne will I be greater than you." And Pharaoh said to Joseph, "See, I have set you over all the land of Egypt." —Genesis 41:39-41

What a turn of events! In little more than a moment, Joseph's position in the natural realm lined up with his spiritual condition of power, authority, favor, and everything God promised him. He was now thirty years old. But since before the age of seventeen he sensed all that was riding on his resilience. He had endured hell and high water, and now, he stood ready.

Once Pharaoh spoke to Joseph, he knew exactly what was at stake. Pharaoh's dreams revealed a larger picture—much more of what God already knew—and proved that Joseph's long uphill battle had been worth it. The fight was for much more than his personal destiny. The survival of entire nations was in play, including that of God's chosen people, Israel.

Joseph was God's man, and with God's anointing, he came to his *kairos* moment, and by the Spirit, he delivered!

THE GARMENT OF DESTINY

Once Joseph delivered God's wisdom to Pharaoh, the grateful ruler marked the moment with highly symbolic actions. These steps expressed his will and ensured Joseph's acceptance by all Egyptians:

> *Pharaoh took his signet ring off his hand and put it on Joseph's hand; and he clothed him in garments of fine linen and put a gold chain around his neck. And he had him ride in the second chariot which he had; and they cried out before him, "Bow the knee!" So he set him over all the land of Egypt. —Genesis 41:42-43*

Pharaoh publicly declared Joseph's high office, not only with words but with meaningful symbols. The signet ring he put on Joseph's hand meant that Pharaoh's authority backed

Joseph's words and actions. As the ring's wearer, Joseph would be obeyed with no questions asked. He would speak on Pharaoh's behalf, and the people (including Pharaoh's entire court) would heed every word as though it had come from Pharaoh's own mouth.

Pharaoh also clothed Joseph in "garments of fine linen and put a gold chain around his neck" (Genesis 41:42). This was a profound act. It had been some time since Joseph had worn finery. Yet, this change of garments altered more than Joseph's outward appearance. Like every other significant change of garments thrust upon Joseph during his lifetime, this one represented a transitional moment in his story.

The first such change in the biblical record involved the coat of many colors that his father Jacob made specially for him (Genesis 37:3). The second change of garments was when Joseph's brothers stripped him of that coat, which had aroused their jealousy and anger (Genesis 37:23). The third change occurred when Potiphar's wife held onto Joseph's coat as he fled her advances (Genesis 39:12). The fourth and final change of garments happened in Genesis 41, when Pharaoh dressed Joseph in fine linens.

Joseph's garments spoke volumes! The coat of many colors proclaimed his father Jacob's favor and foreshadowed Joseph's future authority as head of the family. Joseph's brothers not only stole that coat from him but also desecrated it by soaking it in the blood of an animal. When they presented the stained garment to Jacob as supposed evidence of Joseph's death, it not only spoke of his son's demise but also the shattering of a dream—his dream for his son, his son's dreams for his own future, and (seemingly) God's dreams for Joseph as leader.

Potiphar's wife also used Joseph's coat to perpetrate a lie—not to substantiate his death but to "prove" his guilt. The stripping of the first coat committed Joseph to a life of slavery. This second stripping of his garment would commit him to imprisonment.

When Pharaoh changed Joseph's garments, he dressed Joseph for his future. All previous injustices were undone, and Joseph received his garments of destiny. He became more than the next Jacob and more than Potiphar's man. Joseph was now destined for even greater authority and would serve at a level that was virtually unimaginable for a man in his situation. And no one would ever strip Joseph of his garments again.

OWNING THE CALLING

How could a man with no former political experience (a man who was considered little more than a slave with a prison record) enter this moment as a virtual unknown and end up advising the ruler of Egypt? It was possible because God arranged it and because Joseph kept himself ready. He determined early in life that his relationship with God was more valuable than anything else. From this unshakable perspective, he protected that relationship at all costs.

Joseph diligently attended to his character and to the deposit of the Spirit within him. He kept his heart free of bitterness and kept his spirit free from wrath. If Joseph had compromised or given up, he would not have received his garments of destiny. God sustained Joseph and designed His plan with Joseph's anointing of destination in mind. But only Joseph could own his calling.

And he did. He stayed in intimate relationship with God and made sure his *enchrio* was growing. Therefore, God also granted him an *epichrio* anointing, which he exercised by interpreting dreams for other prisoners and for Pharaoh. You could say that Joseph's *enchrio* unlocked his *epichrio*, and his *epichrio* unlocked the relationship that released the promotion Joseph's dreams foretold in his youth.

The lesson could not be clearer. When the anointing of God is operating in your life, don't let your circumstances sway you. Own your calling and persist in doing exactly what God has prepared you to do. You might be tempted to withdraw into yourself and dwell on the wrongs that people have done to you. You might be consumed by unexpected hardships that have set you back. You might even be stripped of your coat more than once. But don't worry. Your garment of destiny awaits you.

Joseph was tempted in every conceivable way but refused to be defined by negative or tormenting situations. If he had wrapped himself in self-pity and withdrawn himself from the plan of God, he might never have left that prison alive. He might have missed his moment and forfeited the garments of destiny in which Pharaoh now wrapped him.

However, Joseph leaned into God's call and trusted His empowerment. He resisted every blow that was meant to destroy him. Instead of being overwhelmed by his sorrows, he leaned into God's will. Could the younger Joseph have known how important his stand would be? Did he realize the full extent of his future place in history? Probably not. He only knew that God had anointed him to lead, and he nurtured that revelation. He anchored it so deep within his spirit that it drove him closer to God and enabled him to maintain the vision through every storm. When the whole world seemed to turn against him, Joseph continued to own his calling and trust God to do whatever was necessary to bring his *kairos* moment and his prophetic promise to pass.

GOD'S PLAN IS BIGGER

Owning your calling isn't easy, even for a Joseph. What must have seemed to him an exercise in frustration proved to be the exercise of divine preparation. God wasted nothing in Joseph's life—not his gifts, his abilities, his time, or his struggles. God doesn't waste anything in our lives either. We can confidently trust His prophetic promises to unfold in precise order and timing. Then, like Joseph, we can handle the fulfillment without being harmed in any way.

Timing is crucial to divine fulfillment. I'm sure Joseph hoped to get out of prison years earlier and suffered his share of disappointments. But if he had been freed prematurely, he might have become nothing more than a gifted parolee from Egypt's correctional system. Of course, God had much bigger plans for Joseph than that, and Pharaoh was integral to those plans.

God was not only preparing Joseph; He also had to prepare Pharaoh. Prior to their initial encounter, Pharaoh had to experience the dreams that alerted him to his own need.

He had to realize that his power could not protect him from the omen those dreams seemed to represent. Joseph's destiny fulfillment would come into view once Pharaoh's dreams and fears were on the table. Then, God would position Joseph to address Pharaoh's need and enter the prophetic promise.

God's plan is always bigger than we realize. The intricacies of Joseph's story show that God does not sit idly by or ignore our cries. His timing is not random or thoughtless. He is not oblivious or indifferent to our struggles. He not only intends to deliver us; He intends to elevate us into something greater. He systematically grooms us and grows us in maturity and the anointing. He knows what He is doing and what we can handle. We can trust Him! If He has given us prophetic promises, our destiny moments will come. But we have to keep standing. We can't settle for something less. We need to stand until God lifts us into the future He envisions.

God will not fail us. Our moments are coming. The question is, "Will we be ready?"

JOSEPH SOWED AND REAPED

After Pharaoh dressed Joseph in the garments befitting his new office, he publicly described the extent of the power he had bequeathed to Joseph, which must have shocked the members of his court:

> *Pharaoh also said to Joseph, "I am Pharaoh, and without your consent no man may lift his hand or foot in all the land of Egypt." . . . So Joseph went out over all the land of Egypt. —Genesis 41:44-45*

Instantly, Joseph's social and political standing in the land of Egypt changed, not only symbolically but practically. It is unlikely that Joseph saw this precise chain of events coming, but the role to which Pharaoh appointed him resonated with the vision Joseph had carried in his heart. You could say that his vision carried him through his years of tribulation, and the prophetic revelation of his calling enabled him to remain free in his spirit—free enough to hang on until the day of his promotion came.

Joseph had been sowing toward his God-given dreams for a very long time and was tested every step of the way. When people hurt, abused, or accused him, he had to choose how he would respond. Which "seeds" would he sow? Would he open his spirit to anger and bitterness or keep his heart tender before the Lord? Would he seek vengeance on his betrayers or put his fate in God's hands? When people lied against him, would he lash out and demand that they restore his good name? Or would he forgive and pray for them and maintain his integrity before God?

You already know that Joseph kept his heart pure. Not everyone embraced his integrity, but Joseph would not diminish his relationship with God to please his detractors. His often painful choices kept his character and holiness in order, which allowed his destiny to unfold in order too. As he stood before Pharaoh, anyone could have seen that Joseph was more than the "dreamer" his brothers accused him of being. He was more than a man with a gift. He was a man of destiny who had learned to walk in ways that made him respected, trusted, and worthy of great authority.

When God deemed it time to promote Joseph, the power He'd already placed on Joseph's life opened floodgates of favor with Pharaoh and his court. In one amazing moment, Joseph's season of reaping arrived. Therefore, Pharaoh delegated his authority to Joseph and publicly endorsed Joseph's new role. Having received a revelation of his destiny and having yielded to the necessary preparation, Joseph was primed to reach his God-appointed destination. Any opposition that had been mounted against him had to give way, and favor would take its place.

THE MOMENTS BEFORE THE MOMENT

Not everyone is called to serve in places as heady as Pharaoh's court. Nevertheless, I am convinced that each of us is called to the anointed lifestyle and to service in God's kingdom. Whatever our callings might be, we are blessed with the ever-present, indwelling Spirit of God. At times, we might not feel anointed. I doubt that Joseph felt anointed every moment of every day. But he *was* anointed, and so are we. When the anointing is evident, favor follows us as it followed Joseph. Like him, we will make a mark on the world, not solely because we are gifted and capable but primarily because the Anointed One is in us.

When we live as anointed, empowered men and women of God, I believe divinely ordered, strategic, season-changing moments will come. It is our choice to seize them. That means being alert and ready, as Joseph was—ready when the business deal of a lifetime is suddenly thrust upon us; ready when an unexpected opportunity for promotion arises; ready when

God causes us to meet our future mates; ready when souls are on the line or a friend needs consolation; ready when God beckons us toward any aspect of His plan for our lives.

The empowerment needed to seize a particular moment doesn't happen in the moment itself. We are prepared in advance, over time, as we commit to living as anointed vessels of the living God. This empowerment is the culmination of our yielding to the God who knows all things.

Joseph's example reveals the basic principles of faith in God and of the anointing of His Spirit. We see in his life what his example can accomplish in each of us. In his unique way, Joseph teaches us how to handle a life of God-given authority. From him, we learn to be ready for that authority and all that it entails.

Other than Jesus, I cannot think of anyone who exemplifies the anointed life more completely than Joseph does. From his father's house to the pit, and from Potiphar's house to the prison, Joseph stood steadfast in his calling, believing that his destiny moment was still ahead. He was right: it was ahead, and he was ready for it.

KAIROS UNFOLDING

What "coat" was stripped from you, and what did it represent? What "garments" has God granted you, and how do they signify His love and promise to you?

Chapter 10

AUTHORITY TO REIGN

"I will give you the keys of the kingdom of heaven, and
whatever you bind on earth will be bound in heaven, and
whatever you loose on earth will be loosed in heaven."
—Matthew 16:19

When you live an anointed, empowered lifestyle, you come to the place where what was once chaotic becomes clear. Suddenly, all that God has allowed you to learn, endure, and develop finds its preordained fulfillment. Your faithfulness to walk humbly and obediently bears much fruit and you realize that yielding to God's will through the barren times has landed you in a place of authority.

Only God can do this, and when He does, it is marvelous— not only in your eyes but in His. Authority at any level is humbling, however. Good leaders and rulers are people of character and are a blessing to the people for whom they are responsible. Always, they carry their dreams in their hearts, but they never lose their commitment to serve. Good rulers endure; they serve and wait, always seeking to respect and model the life of holiness. Therefore, they prosper, receive favor, and inherit the promises of God.

That was Joseph's experience. Within moments of arriving in Pharaoh's presence, he had completely won the ruler's admiration. In natural terms, the situation could not have been more unlikely. But the glorious outcome did not puzzle the God who divinely orchestrated every detail. Nor did the stunning events upset Joseph's composure. He entered his prophetic promise seamlessly and resisted none of God's plans. Joseph's state of preparedness was such that his rise to power was assured.

Whatever the measure of your rule, whether you are responsible for your family, your church, a business, or some other endeavor, God will empower you to rise to your calling and rule well when your time comes. If you cooperate with Him day by day, He will grant you the composure and presence of mind to enter your prophetic promise knowing that it is yours to receive.

POWER? OR AUTHORITY?

There was a time when I considered the words *power* and *authority* to be nearly interchangeable. Then, the Lord began to reveal a difference that is partly about scale and jurisdiction. When you have power, it applies to a certain realm or territory and is directly connected to your call. If you have a prophetic gift, you are empowered to prophesy in a specific territory to which you are assigned.

When you are anointed of God, He assigns you to prescribed territories but also gives you a measure of authority that covers your use of His delegated power. It encompasses those other smaller territories and much more. When you recognize the authority that comes with God's power and use it, it will impact many additional dynamics of your life and ministry.

Understanding the distinction between power and authority is essential to operating at peak effectiveness. Therefore, a lack of understanding can explain some of the ineffectiveness we see as a body and as individuals. Many of God's people settle for mere power. Because they are not connecting the power of God to the calling of God, they never operate in the fullness of God's destiny for them.

When Jesus told Peter, "I will give you the keys of the kingdom of heaven" (Matthew 16:19), the keys represented the authority to bind and loose. Somewhere along the line, much of the church laid down these keys and relinquished its God-given authority. But God had not changed His mind; He empowered us to rule and reign over spiritual issues in our own lives and in the lives of others. When we operate under the anointing of authority, we become responsible for overseeing whatever affects the future of the part of God's kingdom in which we have been called to rule. This kingly type of anointing calls us to authority in the spiritual realm. It is exactly what God intends us to have and use.

AUTHORITY WITHOUT FEAR

During his time in Egypt, Joseph experienced both sides of the authority "equation." He had a measure of authority in his service to Potiphar and in his role at the prison. But he also lived under the hard edge of Egyptian rule. Pharaoh was a powerful and authoritative man. His position was not meant to be questioned. If you were under his authority, you knew that your opinions and questions had little or no standing. When Joseph claimed his innocence regarding the charges that Potiphar's wife leveled against him, Pharoah's underlings did not consider whether Joseph might be innocent. They simply threw him in jail. Had Pharaoh not dreamed his dreams and freed Joseph for his own purposes, Joseph might have remained in prison 'til his dying day.

The same royal authority that kept Joseph in prison eventually worked for his benefit. When Pharaoh met Joseph, he was moved by the power (the giftedness) he recognized in Joseph's life. Pharaoh did not understand the anointing of the Most High God, but he believed in his people's gods and was open to spiritual things. He also knew authority when he saw it and showered Joseph with almost inexplicable favor and authority—in an instant.

Pharaoh moved decisively to promote Joseph, and Joseph was equally decisive in responding to Pharaoh's favor. Many people would have hesitated to exercise their gifts in such an intimidating setting, especially someone who was abused and rejected at an early age because of those gifts. Some people in today's church hesitate to exercise their gifts in much safer settings. But Joseph recognized both the power and the authority that God had given him. He was neither afraid nor intimidated by Pharaoh. We cannot assess the details of his emotions because the text does not describe them. But Joseph's actions don't reveal fear; they suggest that he was confident in carrying out what he was called to do, even when standing face-to-face with the ruler of Egypt.

If Joseph had withheld his gift for fear of angering or offending Pharaoh, he would have forfeited his moment, along with the favor and strategic position that Pharaoh would soon grant him. In other words, Joseph would have aborted a much larger plan that included Pharaoh, Egypt, the region, and the young nation of Israel.

When God grants us authority, we need to rise to the occasion. We cannot equivocate because we fear what others might say when we exercise the authority God gives us. We are called to make full and proper use of it, even when it displeases others. Then, the goodness of God's will is seen, and He will grant us even greater measures of authority, for His glory.

Joseph knew better than to second-guess himself, cede God's gifts, and return to the dust of the dungeon without apprehending his moment. He knew exactly who he was and who he was becoming. He was gifted and was a godsend to Pharaoh. The royal encounter had been divinely prepared as his opportunity to shine. So, Joseph used his gifts and acted like the man he was on the inside: the man who Pharaoh desperately needed, a man who had the keys to the kingdom in his pocket.

From the moment Pharaoh appointed him, Joseph used his authority prudently and became increasingly indispensable. Over the seven years of plenty and seven years of famine, his interpretation of Pharaoh's dreams proved entirely accurate. Pharaoh's trust in Joseph only grew. He tasked Joseph to handle every aspect of the crisis and address all the people's concerns:

> Then the seven years of plenty which were in the land of Egypt ended, and the seven years of famine began to come, as Joseph had said. The famine was in all lands, but in all the land of Egypt there was bread. So when all the land of Egypt was famished, the people cried to Pharaoh for bread. Then Pharaoh said to all the Egyptians, "Go to Joseph; whatever he says to you, do." —Genesis 41:53-55

Joseph stepped into his role with both feet and with his eyes wide open. He became all that God ordained and all that Pharaoh and Egypt needed. Joseph's power to prosper was never more evident than when he filled Egypt's storehouses with grain during the seven "fat" years and sold it to hungry Egyptians in the lean years. When the famine became "severe in all lands" (Genesis 41:57), Joseph's authority affected those lands: "All countries came to Joseph . . . to buy grain" (Genesis 41:57), and as they did, Egypt was enriched. Joseph was faithful to use the power God gave him. In obedience to the Holy Spirit, he positioned himself for even more authority.

THE ANOINTING WON PHARAOH

Because he perceived the anointing on Joseph, Pharaoh granted him broad authority. He simply liked what he saw in Joseph, and so he favored him. That is how the anointing works on the people around you. Are you anointed? Do you know you are anointed? Have you experienced the power and authority of God in your life? Then you should expect favor to come!

Favor is a basic dynamic of the anointing, but it does not come without preparation. Jesus, the Anointed One, is our ultimate model in every aspect of holy living, and even His favor with God involved preparation. Luke 2:52 says that "Jesus increased in wisdom and stature, and in favor with God and men."

The kind of favor that follows the anointing makes things that are impossible in the natural become possible. That was exactly Joseph's experience throughout his time in Egypt. To give him favor in prison, God had to change the pagan heart of the jailer and awaken him to Joseph's value. When the jailer gave Joseph authority, Joseph did not rest on his laurels. He kept using the gifts God deposited in him, which increased the favor he received. And when the butler failed to remember Joseph to Pharaoh, Joseph did not quench God's anointing by withholding his gifts from others. He was stretched by his trials and probably felt at times that he could stretch no further, but he understood God's prophetic promise to him, and he knew that true favor never comes from people; it comes from God. So, he continued to use his gifts in obedience to God and for the good of others.

When God determined that it was time for Joseph to enter Pharaoh's court, the true source of Joseph's favor was apparent. God had seen Joseph's response in the hard times, and He carefully arranged Joseph's liberation. When the great day came, God blessed Joseph in a big way: He caused the world's most powerful man to proclaim Joseph's far-ranging authority in a very public way. It was a move so radical that we need to take another look:

> *Pharaoh took his signet ring off his hand and put it on Joseph's hand; and he clothed him in garments of fine linen and put a gold chain around his neck. And he had him ride in the second chariot which he had; and they cried out before him, "Bow the knee!" So he set him over all the land of Egypt. Pharaoh also said to Joseph, "I am Pharaoh, and without your consent no man may lift his hand or foot in all the land of Egypt." —Genesis 41:42-44*

Neither Joseph's confidence nor his impressive plan would have won over Pharaoh without the anointing and authority God had granted him. Pharaoh was so taken with Joseph that he made him (a virtual stranger) head over all that he had—with no questions asked of Joseph or of his own advisors.

It was an extreme investment of royal power and authority with far-reaching implications! Because of his new position in Pharaoh's kingdom, Joseph would have authority over everyone but Pharaoh, including all those members of Pharaoh's court who had previously ruled over him. Imagine Potiphar, the chief butler, the jailer, the court magicians, Pharaoh's advisors, and Potiphar's wife having to bow to Joseph!

Joseph could not have orchestrated such a turnaround. Only God, the One who essentially prophesied it, could have brought it to pass. It was not as though Pharaoh gave Joseph a thimbleful of power and authority. His decision was not a mere gesture but a sweeping endorsement of Joseph's role and identity in God. Yes, Pharaoh outranked Joseph, but only in the sense that Pharaoh retained the throne. He delegated all authority to Joseph, and Joseph used it for Pharaoh's benefit.

Joseph had suffered many hard days and long nights. But God never forgot or failed Joseph. Far from it! He kept His promise and vindicated Joseph in the most spectacular way.

THE ANOINTING PREPARED JOSEPH FOR AUTHORITY

Joseph's phenomenal appointment by Pharaoh was possible because God anointed Joseph, and Joseph cooperated with God's anointing. When Pharaoh summoned Joseph from the dungeon and shared his frightening dreams with him, Joseph needed no time to scramble, get his bearings, concoct an answer, or consult his notes. He did not make a lucky guess or check the weather to formulate his recommendation. Joseph simply delivered what God gave him: the truthful interpretation of Pharaoh's dreams.

Because of his anointed lifestyle, Joseph was well-composed and ready to take on the tremendous responsibility Pharaoh delegated to him. When Pharaoh put him on the spot, Joseph did not have to pray down an answer. His anointing for knowing mysteries was part of his everyday life. He was equipped by God to be a man of dreams and interpretations, and he had diligently used his gift. I believe he was also anointed to discern the dynamics of his initial interaction with Pharaoh. God enabled him to read Pharaoh accurately, so he could respond appropriately.

Joseph was so perfectly poised in their exchange that after he answered Pharaoh's questions, he provided answers that

Pharaoh had not sought. He offered guidance about who would manage the famine and how Egypt would be spared destruction. It was as though Joseph arrived with a complete brief, including a clear plan of action and a certain staffing recommendation. Joseph's bold but impromptu presentation manifested his administrative gift and made way for his elevation to power.

Joseph's anointing had prepared him for authority in a setting fraught with hazards. Giving advice to kings is nothing to play with. Those who do it had better know that their advice is sound, or they might lose their heads. Joseph knew Pharaoh's summons wasn't child's play. But he also knew he wasn't stabbing in the dark. He had walked with God and listened for His voice in the good times and the bad. Because of this communion, and because he protected his anointing and his relationship with God, Joseph's prophetic gift was razor-sharp and primed for the moment.

As an anointed vessel of God, you are called to the kind of vivid and fruitful life that Joseph lived. You can also attract favor and receive authority. God will handpick influencers to affirm your gifts and your assignment from God. You are destined to have favor wherever you go. You are called to walk in the burden-removing, yoke-destroying anointing of God. As you do, you will find that people (even rulers of nations) will bless you, even when they don't fully understand why.

JOSEPH'S MOTIVES WERE PURE

Favor, power, and authority are benefits of the anointing—not for self-aggrandizement but for the furthering of the Lord's work. Joseph had been groomed by God for this moment and understood the purpose of his meeting with Pharaoh. It was not only meant to free Joseph from unjust detention. It was part of the divine plan to bless and preserve people and nations, especially Joseph's own people, Israel.

When Pharaoh asked his servants, "Can we find such a one as this, a man in whom is the Spirit of God?" (Genesis 41:38), he was expressing his unequivocal approval of Joseph and all he said and did. Finding people who are both wise and humble is difficult, and Pharaoh was sure he had found both virtues in Joseph.

He was right! Given a moment in Joseph's shoes, most candidates would have seen an opportunity for personal gain. Some would have played on Pharaoh's anxiety to extract some concession or personal favor before agreeing to help him. Pharaoh was no stranger to human motivations. He was a man of vast experience who had learned to examine people's words and find the motives behind them. He knew what most people wanted even before they opened their mouths to speak.

Joseph, however, seemed to be another kind of man. He was anointed and comfortable with authority, but he was not driven by ulterior motives. Pharaoh was clearly in a vulnerable position, being deeply worried and apparently convinced that his dreams were a bad omen. Joseph could easily have leveraged the king's worries and gotten almost anything he wanted from him. But Joseph was not greedy or manipulative. He asked nothing for himself and seemed genuinely interested in the welfare of the Egyptian people. As a result, he impressed a man who was not easily impressed. Pharaoh had met many wise men, and Joseph exceeded them all. He'd also met many slick operators, and he sensed that Joseph was not one of them. There was something different and refreshing about Joseph, and it struck a chord in Pharaoh's heart.

When your heart is pure, God can cause you to flourish in the most imposing and unlikely places. Even when you feel stuck in a low place—even as low as the dungeon—your God-given gifts (His anointing, favor, power, and authority) can remove every barrier and cause you to prosper. Just when you think that God is not moving on your behalf, you can find yourself standing before a "pharaoh" who feels compelled to honor and bless you. He or she can look beyond your circumstances and see in you something indispensable—something they have not seen before and believe they might never see again.

If you think that what happened to Joseph can't happen to you, think again. Regardless of what you have suffered or how long you have languished, someone in high places will see God in you and invest you with power and authority to reign in a setting that you least expect. Just stay ready, and your moment will come. When it does, its suddenness will surprise you but not upset your footing. You will know who you are and *whose* you are because you will have been prepared by the One who also prepared your path. Your destiny is in Him, and it is waiting for you.

YOUR RIGHT TO REIGN

What is the prophetic promise that keeps your heart alert and your eyes fixed on a moment yet to come? Imagine that moment and describe it in written words.

Afterword

THE CAMELS
ARE COMING

*He has sent Me ... to proclaim the acceptable
year of the LORD, and the day of vengeance
of our God; to comfort all who mourn.*
—Isaiah 61:1-2

I began this book by stating that the life of Joseph, Israel's deliverance from Egypt, and their possession of the Promised Land are more than mere historical accounts; they are prophetic oracles to the end-time church. I know that the power of the blood of Christ and the burden-removing, yoke-destroying anointing of the Holy Spirit are essential to possessing the unique callings and destinies we all have.

The journey from bondage to the place of prophetic promise is a trek of experiencing revelations about God and about who we are. That journey will forever change us and mold us into the warriors we are called to be. Only by the power of the blood, prophetic perspective, and living an anointed lifestyle can we conquer the adversaries that are trying to block us from entering our personal places of promise. We are called to be modern-day Joshuas and Josephs, people who refuse to quit—people who know that if God has declared something, it will come to pass, no matter the circumstances.

The generation that ultimately crossed the Jordan with Joshua had a revelation of who they really were and what God had promised them. They also knew there would be a fight to possess it. They arose to the challenge, defeating thirty-one kings and thirty-one teams of mighty men. And, ultimately, they took thirty-one strategic cities. These victories resulted in Israel's taking control of and having peace in the land of promise. As Joshua 11:23 says, "Joshua took the whole land, according to all that the LORD had said to Moses; and Joshua gave it as an inheritance to Israel according to their divisions by their tribes. Then the land rested from war."

To see a rest from war requires a series of progressive actions resulting in total victory over our enemies. We have often lived with something less, thinking that partial victory is as good as it gets. But the idea of settling for just a slice of the proverbial pie is not scriptural. The Word says in Philippians 4:19: "My God shall supply all your need according to His riches in glory by Christ Jesus." God wants victory for you physically, financially, relationally, mentally, emotionally, and (most of all) spiritually. Joshua did not settle for a piece of the pie. The day came when Israel rested from war because thirty-one distinct victories had been won. But their story is not solely about them.

You are on a pathway to total victory.

You are on a pathway to health and prosperity.

You are on a pathway to joy and peace.

You are on a pathway to family revival and restoration.

The lifestyle of the anointed will always be a life of dreams and visions, virtue and holiness, endurance, health, and prosperity. The only person who can stop the fulfillment of your "God said" is *you*! The devil cannot steal your gifts and calling unless you lay them down. Your gifts don't cease to function unless you refuse to stir them. Your journey doesn't stop unless you give up. To rest from your war is not the result of signing a peace treaty with Satan; it is the result of completely overcoming him "by the blood of the Lamb and by the word of [your] testimony" and by not loving your life to the death (Revelation 12:11).

Your rest from war is the result of winning many battles!

This might be the hardest season you have experienced so far. It might seem as though the situation you face will never break. It might even seem as though the situation is breaking you. I know the feeling, but I have lived long enough to know there's another side of the coin. God will not break, and neither will you. He is not worried or surprised by what worries or surprises you. He is, however, compassionate, and He is full of mercy and truth. Whatever He has promised and ordained will come to pass *because* He promised and ordained it. Therefore, you need to rise up and prepare yourself for its arrival.

God said as much to our congregation not long ago. He said, "Everything is coming." That was a confirmation for me, my wife, Gayla, and our whole church. God was speaking to us about a season of recompense, a time of payback. Some things were being set right. Some barriers were coming down. Certain promises were about to be fulfilled, and certain dreams were coming due.

My wife Gayla had already shared a vision about this with our church. She saw a huge camel laden with gold, precious jewels, incense, and other blessings of God. Around the camel's neck was a lanyard with an embroidered identification tag bearing our names. We hadn't ordered anything from Amazon. It wasn't either of our birthdays. FedEx sent us no notice of a coming package. Yet stuff was heading our way, and everything on that camel's back was ours. A season of recompense had arrived.

But there was more. Behind that first camel was a whole caravan of camels. Each one had somebody's name embroidered on its identification tag. Each one carried a pile of blessings for someone in the congregation who was serving faithfully in the church. The Lord's message to us was clear: "The camels are coming! Your names are on them. I'm about to do some very specific things in your lives."

Camels are amazing animals. They will transport people and goods through the driest, hottest terrain. The FedEx van might not make it through the desert sands, but when the camels are carrying your stuff, you can count on their arrival. You don't need a tracking number. You don't have to make any phone calls. All you have to do is wait and receive your delivery. It will not fail.

The word of the Lord about "everything is coming" took our church into the Book of Isaiah. As prophets go, Isaiah articulates the reality of the Lord's coming as powerfully as anyone, and he expresses God's promise to set things right. God said He would "proclaim the acceptable year of the LORD, and the day of vengeance of our God; to comfort all who mourn" (Isaiah 61:2). He promised a day of recompense, and He will deliver.

Isaiah 60 also prophesied along these lines. The following is a familiar passage, but take your time to read and absorb every word:

Arise, shine; for your light has come!
And the glory of the LORD is risen upon you.
For behold, the darkness shall cover the earth,
And deep darkness the people;
But the LORD will arise over you,
And His glory will be seen upon you.
The Gentiles shall come to your light,
And kings to the brightness of your rising.
Lift up your eyes all around, and see:
They all gather together, they come to you;
Your sons shall come from afar,
And your daughters shall be nursed at your side.
Then you shall see and become radiant,
And your heart shall swell with joy;
Because the abundance of the sea shall be turned
to you,
The wealth of the Gentiles shall come to you.
—Isaiah 60:1-5

Recompense! Now, look at verse 6: "The multitude of camels shall cover your *land*, the dromedaries of Midian and Ephah; all those from Sheba shall come; they shall bring gold and incense, and they shall proclaim the praises of the LORD" (Isaiah 60:6).

I want you to hear this in your spirit: *everything is coming—* everything you need to obey the call of God, everything you need to provide for your family, everything He has promised and placed as a desire in your heart—*everything.*

Let me assure you, however, that waiting for His recompense is not a passive act. You have to engage with your payback. I've heard messages preached about "just letting it go." That is not a biblical attitude, in my opinion. When the Amalekites came in, burned down the city, and abducted the wives and children of David and his men, David didn't ask the Lord for the grace to "just let it go."

No! "David and the people who *were* with him lifted up their voices and wept, until they had no more power to weep" (1 Samuel 30:4). Not only were their families gone, but David's grieving men threatened to stone him for it (1 Samuel 30:6). Things could not have been much worse, "but David strengthened himself in the LORD his God" and "inquired of the LORD, saying, 'Shall I pursue this troop? Shall I overtake them?'" (1 Samuel 30:6, 8).

David engaged with God, and God answered him, saying, "Pursue, for you shall surely overtake *them* and without fail recover *all*" (1 Samuel 30:8). David and his men were not about to give up on their loved ones. They were unwilling to let the atrocity go. The Amalekites would not have the last word.

David and his men had a word from God, and they acted on it. Their day of recompense came, and they recovered what the Amalekites had stolen.

Let me remind you of something else that God has said: "The thief does not come except to steal, and to kill, and to destroy. I have come that they may have life, and that they may have *it* more abundantly" (John 10:10). Instead of slipping into a spiritually passive mentality and accepting what we are handed, we need to arise like David did—like the sons and daughters of God that we are. It's time to say, "We are going to get it all back!"

If the enemy has stolen anything from you—and I mean *anything*—then you are on God's schedule for recompense. "The multitude of camels shall cover your *land*" (Isaiah 60:6). Payback is coming to you, and the enemy will get the retribution he has coming. The salvation of the Lord is on the way. Isaiah 60:1 does not say that you have to come to the light; it says the light is coming to you. Recompense is coming to you as surely as it came to Joseph in the dungeon. So, scan the horizon. The camels are coming!

I believe there is coming a restoration of families in the church. I'm not talking about one of your children being saved and three going their own way. I'm talking about whole families coming into the kingdom. God is determined to bring blessing, and nothing can stop it. God doesn't care what is standing between you and your blessing. There may be hundreds of miles of desert to cover. But the camels can handle it. They can drink twenty-six gallons of water in ten minutes and because they store fat reserves in their humps, they can survive up to two weeks without food. Those great beasts can run at 40 mph in the desert. They will get to you!

God has a way of traversing the deserts in our lives. He has the spiritual camels and all the necessary gear in His spiritual arsenal. It is no problem for Him to load up the camels and send you whatever He has declared is yours. Have His blessings been prophesied to you? Then, there is already a camel with your name on it. Have you had some dreams like Joseph did or some visions of things that God wants to do for your family or career? There is a camel with your name on it. What God loads onto your camel might be different from what He prepares for someone else. But it's *your* camel, and it is carrying what God says is yours.

It doesn't matter how big your desert is. The mighty Sahara cannot intimidate God. When He sends the camels, you can be sure they will arrive.

Meanwhile, this is my prayer for you:

Heavenly Father,
I pray that the revelation of who You are will fill the
minds of all who have read this book. I pray that the
revelation of who they are and the knowledge of their
gifts and callings will reside deep in their spirits. I
claim an anointed lifestyle for the rest of their lives.
I plead the blood of the Lamb over the doorway of
their hearts so that the destroyer is paralyzed and
unable to harm them or their families. I thank You,
God, that they will defeat the adversaries of their
destinies and will have rest and peace from war.
I thank You that their camels are en route to
supply any and all needs, with overflow. I thank
You that they will walk in total victory—body,
soul, and spirit. In the name of Jesus, I pray!

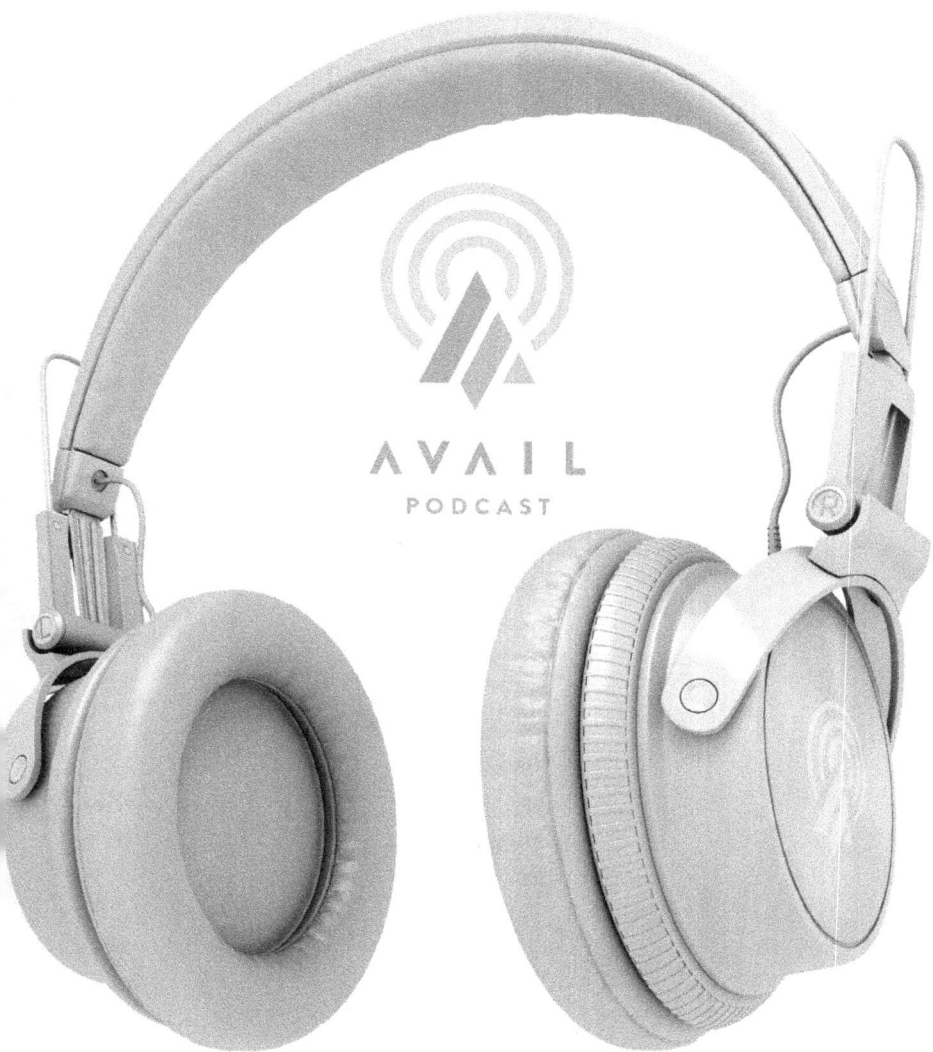

AVAIL
PODCAST

LISTEN WHEREVER YOU GET YOUR PODCASTS
AVAIL LEADERSHIP PODCAST

FOLLOW THE LEADER

STAY CONNECTED

facebook.com/TheArtofAvail   @theartofavail   AVAIL

www.ingramcontent.com/pod-product-compliance
Lightning Source LLC
Chambersburg PA
CBHW070535090426
42735CB00013B/2986